Test Prep

Grade 7

Test Preparation for:

Reading
Language
Math

Program Authors:
Dale Foreman
Alan C. Cohen
Jerome D. Kaplan
Ruth Mitchell

Table of Contents

Send all inquiries to:
McGraw-Hill Children's Publishing
8787 Orion Place
Columbus, OH 43240-4027

1-56189-757-4

2 3 4 5 6 7 8 9 10 PHXBK 05 04 03 02

Test Prep

The Program That Teaches Test-Taking Achievement

For over two decades, McGraw-Hill has helped students perform their best when taking standardized achievement tests. Over the years, we have identified the skills and strategies that students need to master the challenges of taking a standardized test. Becoming familiar with the test-taking experience can help ensure your child's success.

Test Prep covers all test skill areas

Test Prep contains the subject areas that are represented in the five major standardized tests. *Test Prep* will help your child prepare for the following tests:

- California Achievement Tests® (CAT/5)
- Comprehensive Tests of Basic Skills (CTBS/4)
- Iowa Tests of Basic Skills® (ITBS, Form K)
- Metropolitan Achievement Test (MAT/7)
- Stanford Achievement Test(SAT/9)

Test Prep provides strategies for success

Many students need special support when preparing to take a standardized test. *Test Prep* gives your child the opportunity to practice and become familiar with:

- General test content
- The test format
- Listening and following standard directions
- Working in structured settings
- Maintaining a silent, sustained effort
- Using test-taking strategies

Test Prep is comprehensive

Test Prep Provides a complete presentation of the types of skills covered in standardized tests in a variety of formats. These formats are similar to those your child will encounter when testing. The subject areas covered in this book include:

- Reading
- Language
- Math

Test Prep gives students the practice they need

Each student lesson provides several components that help develop test-taking skills:

- An **Example,** with directions and sample test items
- A **Tips** feature, that give test-taking strategies
- A **Practice** section, to help students practice answering questions in each test format

Each book gives focused test practice that builds confidence:

- A **Test Yourself** lesson for each unit gives students the opportunity to apply what they have learned in the unit
- A **Test Practice** section gives students the experience of a longer test-like situation.
- A **Progress Chart** for students to note and record their own progress.

Test Prep is the first and most successful program ever developed to help students become familiar with the test-taking experience. *Test Prep* can help to build self-confidence, reduce test anxiety, and provide the opportunity for students to successfully show what they have learned.

A Message to Parents and Teachers:

- **Standardized tests: the yardstick for your child's future**

  Standardized testing is one of the cornerstones of American education. From its beginning in the early part of this century, standardized testing has gradually become the yardstick by which student performance is judged. For better or worse, your child's future will be determined in great part by how well he or she performs on the standardized test used by your school district.

- **Even good students can have trouble with testing**

  In general, standardized tests are well designed and carefully developed to assess students' abilities in a consistent and balanced manner. However, there are many factors that can hinder the performance of an individual student when testing. These might include test anxiety, unfamiliarity with the test's format, or failure to understand the directions.

  In addition, it is rare that students are taught all of the material that appears on a standardized test. This is because the curriculum of most schools does not directly match the content of the standardized test. There will certainly be overlap between what your child learns in school and how he or she is tested, but some materials will probably be unfamiliar.

- **Ready to Test will lend a helping hand**

  It is because of the shortcomings of the standardized testing process that *Test Prep* was developed. The lessons in the book were created after a careful analysis of the most popular achievement tests. The items, while different from those on the tests, reflect the types of material that your child will encounter when testing. Students who use *Test Prep* will also become familiar with the format of the most popular achievement tests. This learning experience will reduce anxiety and give your child the opportunity to do his or her best on the next standardized test.

We urge you to review with your child the Message to Students and the feature "How to Use This Book" on pages 7-8. The information on these pages will help your child to use this book and develop important test-taking skills. We are confident that following the recommendations in this book will help your child to earn a test score that accurately reflects his or her true ability.

A Message to Students:

Frequently in school you will be asked to take a standardized achievement test. This test will show how much you know compared to other students in your grade. Your score on a standardized achievement test will help your teachers plan your education. It will also give you and your parents an idea of what your learning strengths and weaknesses are.

This book will help you do your best on a standardized achievement test. It will show you what to expect on the test and will give you a chance to practice important reading and test-taking skills. Here are some suggestions you can follow to make the best use of *Test Prep*.

Plan for success

- You'll do your best if you begin studying and do one or two lessons in this book each week. If you only have a little bit of time before a test is given, you can do one or two lessons each day.
- Study a little bit at a time, no more than 30 minutes a day. If you can, choose the same time each day to study in a quiet place.
- Keep a record of your score on each lesson. The charts on pp. 154–156 of this book will help you do this.

On the day of the test . . .

- Get a good night's sleep the night before the test. Have a light breakfast and lunch to keep from feeling drowsy during the test.
- Use the tips you learned in *Test Prep*. The most important tips are to skip difficult items, take the best guess when you're unsure of the answer, and try all the items.
- Don't worry if you are a little nervous when you take an achievement test. This is a natural feeling and may even help you stay alert.

How to Use This Book

1 *Getting Started*

Read the directions carefully.

Do the Sample item(s).

Read the Tip(s).

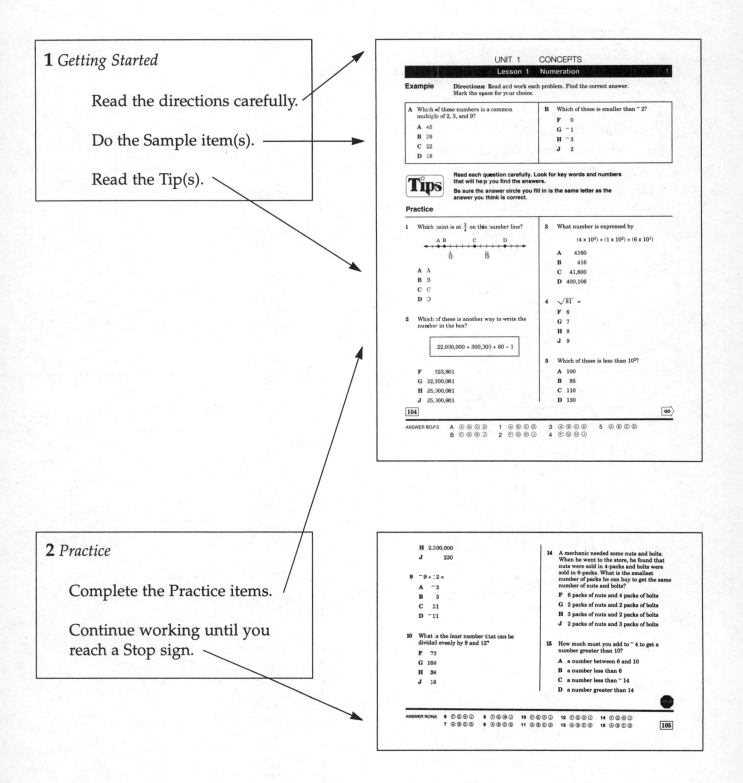

2 *Practice*

Complete the Practice items.

Continue working until you reach a Stop sign.

3 *Check It Out*

Check your answers by turning to the Answer Key at the back of the book.

Keep track of how you're doing by marking the number right on the Progress Charts on pages 154-156.

Mark the lesson you completed on the table of contents for each section.

Answer Keys

Reading Unit 1, Vocabulary

Lesson 1
A B
B J
1 B
2 H
3 D
4 F
5 D
6 G
7 A
8 G

Lesson 2
A A
B H
1 C
2 G
3 A
4 J
5 C
6 F
7 B

Lesson 3
A D
B G
1 D
2 G
3 A
4 H
5 D
6 F
7 C
8 H

Lesson 4
A C
B F
1 A
2 H
3 D
4 J
5 C

Lesson 5
A C
B F
1 D
2 F
3 B
4 H
5 A
6 J

Lesson 6
A B
B J
1 A
2 H
3 D
4 G
5 B

Lesson 7
E1 A
E2 H
1 C
2 J
3 B
4 G
5 D
6 H
7 B
8 F
9 A
10 J
11 B
12 J
13 C
14 F
15 C
16 J
17 A
18 J
19 B
20 J
21 B
22 H
23 C
24 J
25 A
26 J
27 D
28 H
29 D
30 G
31 A
32 J
33 B
34 H

Unit 2, Comprehension

Lesson 8
A A
1 D
2 H
3 B
4 F

Lesson 9
A B
1 D
2 F
3 C
4 G
5 B
6 F
7 C
8 H
9 A
10 H
11 D
12 G
13 D
14 F

Lesson 10
A C
1 D
2 G
3 D
4 G
5 D
6 F
7 A
8 H
9 D
10 J
11 B
12 G
13 B
14 G
15 D
16 G
17 D
18 F
19 C

Lesson 11
E1 B
1 B
2 J
3 A
4 H
5 C
6 J
7 A
8 J
9 B
10 F
11 D
12 H
13 A
14 G
15 A
16 J
17 D
18 F
19 B
20 H
21 A
22 G
23 C
24 F
25 D
26 G
27 C
28 F
29 C
30 H
31 G

Test Practice Part 1
E1 A
E2 H
1 D
2 G

149

Reading Progress Chart

Circle your score for each lesson. Connect your scores to see how well you are doing.

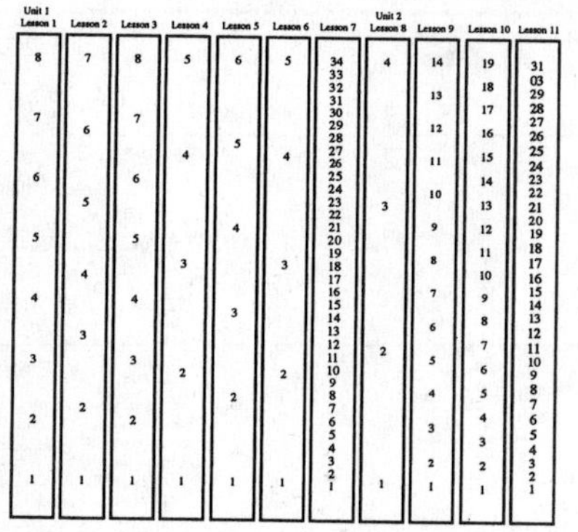

154

Table of Contents

Reading

11

Skills

Reading

VOCABULARY

Identifying synonyms
Identifying words with similar meanings
Identifying antonyms
Identifying multi-meaning words

Identifying words in paragraph context
Identifying word meaning from a clue
Identifying words from a defining statement

READING COMPREHENSION

Recognizing story structures
Differentiating between fact and opinion
Understanding literary devices
Identifying story genres
Recognizing details
Understanding events
Drawing conclusions
Applying story information
Deriving word or phrase meaning
Understanding characters

Sequencing ideas
Making inferences
Making comparisons
Generalizing from story information
Predicting from story content
Choosing the best title for a story
Using a story web
Understanding the author's purpose
Understanding feelings
Understanding the main idea

Language

LANGUAGE MECHANICS

Identifying the need for capital letters (proper
    nouns, beginning words) in sentences
Identifying the need for punctuation marks
    in sentence

Identifying the need for capital letters and
    punctuation marks in printed text

LANGUAGE EXPRESSION

Identifying the correct forms of nouns,
    pronouns, verbs, and adjectives
Recognizing double negatives
Identifying correctly formed sentences

Identifying the correct sentence to complete
    a paragraph
Identifying sentences that do not fit in
    a paragraph
Prewriting

SPELLING

Identifying correctly spelled words
Identifying incorrectly spelled words

STUDY SKILLS

Using a table of contents
Understanding a map
Using a picture dictionary
Alphabetizing words

Math

COMPUTATION

Adding whole numbers, decimals, and fractions
Dividing whole numbers

Multiplying whole numbers
Subtracting whole numbers, decimals,
    and fractions

CONCEPTS

Associating numerals and number words
Comparing and ordering fractions and decimals
Comparing and ordering whole numbers
Converting between decimals and fractions
Estimating
Factoring numbers
Finding multiples
Identifying fractional parts
Naming numerals
Recognizing equivalent fractions
Recognizing odd and even numbers
Recognizing visual and numeric patterns

Reducing fractions
Regrouping
Rounding
Understanding function tables
Understanding number sentences and simple
    equations
Understanding place value
Understanding ratio and proportion
Using a number line
Using a number line with fractions and decimals
Using expanded notation
Using operational symbols, words, properties

APPLICATIONS

Estimating weight and size
Finding perimeter and area
Formulating simple number sentences
Identifying information needed to solve a problem
Reading a calendar
Reading a thermometer
Recognizing plane and solid figures and their
    characteristics
Recognizing value of money and money notation
Solving word problems

Understanding bar graphs and pictographs
Understanding parallel lines
Understanding probability and averages
Understanding spatial relations, congruence and
    symmetry
Understanding tables and charts
Understanding time concepts
Using a coordinate graph
Using standard and metric units of measurement

Strategies

Following group directions
Adjusting to a structured setting
Utilizing test formats
Maintaining a silent, sustained effort
Locating questions and answer choices
Managing time effectively
Considering every answer choice
Noting the lettering of answer choices
Recalling word meanings
Taking the best guess when unsure of the answer
Avoiding overanalysis of answer choices
Skipping difficult items and returning to them later
Identifying the best test-taking strategy
Working methodically
Comparing answer choices
Eliminating answer choices
Checking answer choices
Referring to a passage to find the correct answer
Using logic
Recalling the elements of a correctly formed sentence
Locating the correct answer
Identifying and using key words, figures,
    and numbers
Recalling the elements of a correctly
    formed paragraph

Marking the right answer as soon as it is found
Understanding unusual item formats
Following complex directions
Trying out answer choices
Using context to find the answer
Inferring word meaning from sentence context
Converting problems to a workable format
Staying with the first answer
Previewing items
Responding to items according to difficulty
Finding the answer without computing
Analyzing questions
Identifying and using key words to find the
    answer
Skimming a passage
Referring to a passage to answer questions
Indicating that the correct answer is not given
Using strategic reading techniques
Indicating that an item has no mistakes
Evaluating answer choices
Referring to a reference source
Checking answers by the opposite operation
Performing the correct operation
Reworking a problem
Computing carefully

Table of Contents
Reading

Lesson 1   Synonyms

Examples   **Directions:** Read each item. Choose the word that means the same or about the same as the underlined word.

A beautiful <u>dwelling</u>	**B** A <u>hearty</u> meal is —
A painting	**F** expensive
B house	**G** small
C park	**H** late
D statue	**J** nourishing

 Think about where you heard or read the underlined word before. Try to remember what the word meant before.

If you aren't sure which answer is correct, take your best guess.

Practice

1   <u>reside</u> in Montana

   A visit
   B live
   C arrive
   D hunt

2   <u>satisfactory</u> answer

   F incorrect
   G long
   H acceptable
   J irrelevant

3   <u>hostile</u> force

   A allied
   B retreating
   C immense
   D unfriendly

4   <u>magnificent</u> building

   F fabulous
   G tall
   H occupied
   J vacant

5   An <u>impartial</u> judgment is —

   A angry
   B sensible
   C hasty
   D neutral

6   To <u>resume</u> a trip is to—

   F cancel
   G continue
   H enjoy
   J conclude

7   <u>Periodically</u> means —

   A sometimes
   B always
   C never
   D frequently

8   To <u>detach</u> is to —

   F mail
   G separate
   H fill in
   J throw away

STOP

Examples   **Directions:** Read each item. Choose the answer that means the same or about the same as the underlined word.

A **Become inactive**

A not active
B not present
C not paid
D not friendly

B **Parking is scarce here.**

Scarce means —

F for residents only
G easy to find
H hard to find
J against the law

If an answer is too difficult, skip it and move on to the next item. Come back to the skipped items later.

Practice

1 **A huge freighter**

A passenger train
B jet plane
C cargo ship
D pack horse

2 **Mislead the public**

F give correct information to
G give wrong information to
H govern
J control

3 **Tedious work**

A long and tiring
B paying poorly
C paying well
D short and exciting

4 **Pretend to be sad**

F try to avoid
G act truly
H enjoy
J make believe

5 **The family was stunned by the news.**

Stunned means —

A pleased
B amused
C shocked
D annoyed

6 **Check the gauge on the engine.**

A gauge is —

F a measuring instrument
G a kind of valve
H the fuel level
J a kind of large bolt

7 **They assured us the number was right.**

Assured means —

A told
B promised
C convinced
D warned

STOP

ANSWER ROWS   **A** Ⓐ Ⓑ Ⓒ Ⓓ   **1** Ⓐ Ⓑ Ⓒ Ⓓ   **3** Ⓐ Ⓑ Ⓒ Ⓓ   **5** Ⓐ Ⓑ Ⓒ Ⓓ   **7** Ⓐ Ⓑ Ⓒ Ⓓ
             B Ⓕ Ⓖ Ⓗ Ⓙ   **2** Ⓕ Ⓖ Ⓗ Ⓙ   **4** Ⓕ Ⓖ Ⓗ Ⓙ   **6** Ⓕ Ⓖ Ⓗ Ⓙ

Examples   **Directions:** Read each item. Choose the answer that means the opposite of the underlined word.

A **novice** sailor	B **vast** forest
A skilled	F large
B lost	G tiny
C inexperienced	H ancient
D experienced	J dark

Remember, you are supposed to find the answer that means the opposite of the underlined word.

Practice

1   ambitious person

A   eager
B   diligent
C   intelligent
D   lazy

2   neglect duties

F   ignore
G   perform
H   avoid
J   follow

3   alert guard

A   inattentive
B   watchful
C   volunteer
D   capable

4   sincere apology

F   honest
G   humble
H   false
J   extensive

5   feel sluggish

A   happy
B   unkind
C   unwelcome
D   energetic

6   flimsy package

F   strong
G   weak
H   empty
J   full

7   elegant party

A   loud
B   very exciting
C   informal
D   very crowded

8   delay making a decision

F   put off
G   enjoy
H   decide quickly
J   hate to

STOP

Examples   Directions: Read each item. Choose the answer you think is correct.

A | We will pay a <u>toll</u> on this road. |

In which sentence does the word <u>toll</u> mean the same thing as in the sentence above?

A   The bell will <u>toll</u> in a few minutes.
B   The heat took a <u>toll</u> on the runners.
C   Do you have a quarter for the <u>toll</u>?
D   Overeating takes a <u>toll</u> on a person.

Read both sentences. Choose the word that fits best in both sentences.

B   Be careful when you start or the car will _____ .

Put the horse in the _____ when you have finished riding.

F   stall
G   speed
H   barn
J   ring

Use the meaning of the sentences to find the right answer.

Practice

1 | Her <u>account</u> has fifty dollars in it. |

In which sentence does the word <u>account</u> mean the same thing as in the sentence above?

A   We will check your bank <u>account</u> first.

B   How did he <u>account</u> for the error?

C   Jed lost but gave a good <u>account</u> of himself.

D   The judges took many things into <u>account</u> before awarding the prize.

2 | The <u>conductor</u> asked for our tickets. |

In which sentence does the word <u>conductor</u> mean the same thing as in the sentence above?

F   Silver is a better <u>conductor</u> than copper.

G   The <u>conductor</u> led the school orchestra.

H   Does every train have a <u>conductor</u>?

J   A good <u>conductor</u> is necessary to transmit electricity.

3   The storm won't _____ to much.

The _____ you saved is surprising.

A   come
B   money
C   effort
D   amount

4   An army _____ is near our town.

A large _____ held up the roof.

F   fort
G   log
H   base
J   post

5   Can we _____ that peak?

This _____ is not accurate.

A   climb
B   ruler
C   scale
D   hike

STOP

ANSWER ROWS   A ⒶⒷⒸⒹ   1 ⒶⒷⒸⒹ   3 ⒶⒷⒸⒹ   5 ⒶⒷⒸⒹ
              B ⒻⒼⒽⒿ   2 ⒻⒼⒽⒿ   4 ⒻⒼⒽⒿ

Examples   **Directions:** Read the paragraph. Find the word below the paragraph that fits best in each numbered blank.

Young people today enjoy many high tech ____(A)____ activities like handheld electronic games. Even so, one of the most popular activities is mountain biking, a sport that is growing at a ____(B)____ rate.

A A educational	**B** F remarkable
B financial	G diminishing
C recreational	H responsive
D ineffective	J perceptual

 **Stay with the first answer choice. Change it only if you are sure it is wrong and another answer is better.**

Practice

Having a car ____(1)____ or repaired today is very different from what it was just a few years ago. In the past, most auto parts were ____(2)____ , and could be repaired or replaced without too much difficulty. Many repairs could even be ____(3)____ by automobile owners.

Today's new cars, however, have many electronic ____(4)____ . To track down a problem, the service ____(5)____ plugs the car into a computer! The computer ____(6)____ the problem, suggests repairs, and even provides inventory numbers for parts that have to be replaced.

1 A built	**4** F estimates
B purchased	G visitations
C inserted	H components
D serviced	J measurements
2 F mechanical	**5** A technician
G damaged	B inspection
H installed	C condition
J expensive	D finalist
3 A removed	**6** F causes
B completed	G refines
C avoided	H disallows
D salaried	J diagnoses

STOP

Examples　　**Directions:** Read each question. Fill in the circle for the answer you think is correct.

A Which of these words probably comes from the Dutch word *huid* meaning *skin*?

  A human
  B hide
  C rude
  D fluid

B The workers were _____ in their efforts to repair the dam.

Which of these words would indicate the workers did their best?

  F unusual
  G detained
  H uninvited
  J tireless

 Skim all the questions first. Begin by answering the ones you think are easiest. Then go back and answer the ones that you think are more difficult.

Practice

1 Which of these words probably comes from the Latin word *pistus* meaning *to pound*?

  A piston
  B picture
  C poison
  D spite

2 Which of these words probably comes from the Middle English word *curiosus* meaning *inquisitive*?

  F furious
  G current
  H curious
  J create

3 Which of these words probably comes from the Latin word *sanus* meaning *healthy*?

  A stain
  B sand
  C scare
  D sane

4 They made an _____ decision to build the new highway.

Which of these words means the decision couldn't be changed?

  F influential
  G irrevocable
  H opinionated
  J unsightly

5 The effects of the storm were _____ the next morning.

Which of these words means the effects of the storm could easily be seen?

  A devoted
  B evident
  C respectable
  D affectionate

STOP

ANSWER ROWS　**A** Ⓐ Ⓑ Ⓒ Ⓓ　　**1** Ⓐ Ⓑ Ⓒ Ⓓ　　**3** Ⓐ Ⓑ Ⓒ Ⓓ　　**5** Ⓐ Ⓑ Ⓒ Ⓓ

　　　　　　　B Ⓕ Ⓖ Ⓗ Ⓙ　　**2** Ⓕ Ⓖ Ⓗ Ⓙ　　**4** Ⓕ Ⓖ Ⓗ Ⓙ

Examples

Directions: For E1, choose the word that means the same or almost the same as the underlined word. Mark the correct answer. For E2, read the question. Choose the answer you think is correct.

Which word means the same or almost the same as the underlined word?	E2 Which of these probably comes from the Old English word *pagyn* meaning a *stage*?
E1 find the **origin** **A** beginning **B** end **C** middle **D** opposite	**F** page **G** parlor **H** pageant **J** apparent

For numbers 1-8, find the word or words that mean the same or almost the same as the underlined word.

1 feel compassion

A great joy
B much confusion
C deep sympathy
D nothing at all

2 have a routine day

F unusual
G busy
H profitable
J typical

3 a willing assistant

A unhappy to help
B happy to help
C too busy to help
D unable to help

4 unexpected result

F anticipated
G surprising
H positive
J enjoyable

5 To advise a friend is to —

A hope to avoid
B try to find
C enjoy the company of
D give advice to

6 Contrary opinions are —

F similar
G identical
H opposite
G unfamiliar

7 A hectic schedule is —

A dull
B busy
C quiet
D restful

8 To brood about something is to —

F be unhappy
G be excited
H be unsure
J be happy

GO

9 The hotel was <u>demolished</u> last week.

Demolished means —

A destroyed
B crowded
C completed
D started

10 Their <u>journey</u> around the world lasted more than a year.

A <u>journey</u> is a —

F project
G competition
H famine
J trip

11 People used to <u>barter</u> for necessities.

Barter means —

A argue
B trade
C wish
D pay

12 The room was <u>cramped</u> but pleasant.

Cramped means —

F rented
G spacious
H expensive
J crowded

13 Don't forget to <u>endorse</u> the check before you cash it.

Endorse means —

A spend
B lose
C sign
D cash

For numbers 14-19, find the word that means the opposite of the underlined word.

14 cause <u>distress</u>

F joy
G confusion
H sorrow
J anxiety

15 <u>mention</u> an idea

A disagree with
B insist on
C discuss in depth
D suggest briefly

16 <u>similar</u> experience

F comparable
G superior
H false
J unlike

17 <u>lenient</u> rules

A strict
B unacceptable
C frightening
D surprising

18 <u>emphasize</u> a point

F maximize
G stress
H refine
J minimize

19 <u>intense</u> feelings

A empty
B weak
C strong
D irate

GO

ANSWER ROWS   **9** Ⓐ Ⓑ Ⓒ Ⓓ   **11** Ⓐ Ⓑ Ⓒ Ⓓ   **13** Ⓐ Ⓑ Ⓒ Ⓓ   **15** Ⓐ Ⓑ Ⓒ Ⓓ   **17** Ⓐ Ⓑ Ⓒ Ⓓ   **19** Ⓐ Ⓑ Ⓒ Ⓓ
10 Ⓕ Ⓖ Ⓗ Ⓙ   **12** Ⓕ Ⓖ Ⓗ Ⓙ   **14** Ⓕ Ⓖ Ⓗ Ⓙ   **16** Ⓕ Ⓖ Ⓗ Ⓙ   **18** Ⓕ Ⓖ Ⓗ Ⓙ

19

For numbers 20-23, choose the word that correctly completes <u>both</u> sentences.

20 The _____ on the bed was made by my cousin.

Remember to _____ the paint evenly.

F quilt
G apply
H sheet
J spread

21 I want to _____ how important this meeting is.

Some jobs cause lots of _____ .

A say
B stress
C problems
D indicate

22 The berry _____ is beside the garden.

Sheila had to _____ the tire on her mountain bike.

F repair
G plant
H patch
J bush

23 What is the _____ of that book?

Where is the _____ to the car?

A name
B key
C title
D cost

24 | Please <u>hold</u> this box while I tie my shoe. |

In which sentence does the word <u>hold</u> mean the same thing as in the sentence above?

F The ship's <u>hold</u> filled with water.

G Helen didn't know how much trash the bag would <u>hold</u>.

H <u>Hold</u> off on making the decision until we get more information.

J I can't <u>hold</u> onto this rope much longer.

25 | The <u>present</u> road is in awful shape. |

In which sentence does the word <u>present</u> mean the same thing as in the sentence above?

A The people thought the <u>present</u> mayor was doing a good job.

B The <u>present</u> you sent us just arrived.

C She had a chance to <u>present</u> her ideas to the school board.

D The <u>present</u> is different from the past.

26 | Make a <u>table</u> with the game times. |

In which sentence does the word <u>table</u> mean the same thing as in the sentence above?

F Put the package on the <u>table</u>.

G The committee decided to <u>table</u> the motion.

H Ancient people sometimes wrote on a <u>table</u> of clay.

J This <u>table</u> shows the cost of each car.

GO ⟩

27 Which of these words probably comes from the Latin word *rusticus* meaning *in the country*?

A ruler
B rush
C relic
D rustic

28 Which of these words probably comes from the Old Norse word *gasa* meaning *to stare*?

F gasp
G grasp
H gaze
J graze

29 Cassandra is _____ about the weather.

Which of these words means Cassandra is worried about the weather?

A obstinate
B allocated
C militant
D concerned

30 The team played _____ throughout the whole season.

Which of these words means the team's play was not steady?

F enthusiastically
G inconsistently
H capably
J realistically

Read the paragraph. Find the word below the paragraph that fits best in each numbered blank.

American businesses today are ____(31)____ many changes to remain ____(32)____ in the world marketplace. A common name for the process is "downsizing" because large companies are ____(33)____ unprofitable divisions and are becoming smaller. The goals of downsizing are to increase profits and to provide better products and services. An ____(34)____ effect of downsizing is that some workers lose their jobs.

31 A undergoing
B avoiding
C challenging
D expressing

32 F inanimate
G transferred
H misrepresented
J competitive

33 A acquiring
B shedding
C emphasizing
D mending

34 F elevated
G assimilated
H unfortunate
J influential

STOP

Example   **Directions:** Read each item. Choose the answer you think is correct. Mark the space for your answer.

After school, Jarod and his friends raced out the door and over to the bike rack. When they got there, all of them stared in shock. Both tires on every bike were flat. The kids were speechless, and no one had any idea about what had happened.	**A What part of a story does this passage tell about?** A the plot B the characters C the mood D the setting

Tips   Look for key words in the question. These key words will help you understand the question and find the right answer.

Practice

1   Which of these is an opinion?

A The overnight temperature was 21°.

B Three inches of snow fell yesterday.

C Four people were injured in weather-related accidents.

D The people of the town agreed this was the worst weather in years.

2   The wide-eyed children stood on the beach and stared at the ocean. They had never seen so much water before.

Which of these best explains the meaning of the phrase "wide-eyed children"?

F The sun on the ocean was so bright it hurt their eyes.

G Sand from the beach was blowing into their eyes.

H They couldn't believe what they were seeing.

J They wondered why so much water was in one place.

3   The Himalayas are sometimes called the tallest mountains on earth. The truth is that several underwater ranges are even higher.

A passage like this would most likely be found in a book of —

A fables.

B facts.

C tall tales.

D adventure stories.

4   Which of these statements makes use of a metaphor?

F The mountains were sentinels, guarding the lake and the small farm.

G The bleating of the sheep led us to a hidden canyon.

H The road switched back and forth several times before it reached the summit.

J The river was a ribbon of silver stretched across the plains.

STOP

Example   **Directions:** Read each passage. Find the best answer to the questions that follow the passage.

Gardeners often look to nature for their seeds. In the fall, they collect seeds from wildflowers they admire. Then they either sow the seeds in their gardens or keep them until spring. Wildflowers grown from seed require less water than cultivated flowers and can grow in almost any soil.	**A Gardeners usually collect wildflower seeds in the —** A summer. B fall. C winter. D spring.

 **Skim the passage, then look at the questions. Answer the easiest questions first. Then do the more difficult questions.**

Practice

Here is a passage about an unusual job. Read the passage and then do numbers 1 through 7 on page 24.

They ride bicycles and get paid for it.

Bicycling is done mostly for sport, pleasure, and healthful exercise here in America. Some young people, however, ride bicycles as part of their job. They are city bicycle messengers.

In today's world of faxes, telephones, and computers, you might think that hand delivery of messages or packages is strange. But in cities where downtown traffic is heavily congested, bicycle messengers are doing a thriving business. Delivery by cars and trucks works well in the suburbs, but in the city, nothing beats a bicycle.

Messengers on a bicycle carry many different things. Some items or messages are private, and senders don't want them to be sent by fax. Others are very valuable and it is important that they be carried as quickly as possible from one place to another. Finally, messengers carry important things that can't be transmitted electronically, such as parts for computers or medical laboratory samples.

Bicycles are fast and *maneuverable* in traffic. A car could be tied up in heavy city traffic for hours. A bicycle, because it is smaller, can move through traffic much faster and more easily than a larger vehicle. Bicycles can also go faster than a person walking on city streets.

Few people would brave the dangers of riding through city traffic for pleasure. Those who do this for a living, however, provide a valuable service for both businesses and individuals.

GO

1 **A bicycle messenger's job is to —**

A deliver faxes and mail in large cities with heavy traffic.

B be a daredevil and do dangerous tricks on a bicycle.

C show skill and daring by passing cars and trucks.

D carry messages or small packages through large cities.

2 **Bicycle messengers are best suited for work in —**

F large cities with heavy traffic.

G cities with bicycle lanes.

H suburbs where traffic is light.

J rural areas with wide roads.

3 **To use a bicycle messenger, a company should do all of these *except* —**

A ship documents that could be carried in an envelope.

B give the messenger clear directions and the right address.

C ship a very large package that is difficult to carry.

D keep a record of the package that has been shipped.

4 **Bicycle messengers must —**

F know what is in every envelope they carry.

G know their way around the city very well.

H open the packages they deliver and look inside.

J drive through city parks so they can enjoy the scenery.

5 **You can tell from this passage that the word *maneuverable* means —**

A heavy traffic.

B easily steered.

C very fast.

D somewhat dangerous.

6 **Which of these would make the most sense to send by bicycle messenger?**

F A business contract

G A large computer system

H A desk

J A restaurant menu

7 **Not many people —**

A send important documents in the city.

B know how to ride a bicycle.

C ride through heavy traffic for pleasure.

D send laboratory samples.

GO

The Lesson in the Garden

Miranda did not want to spend her Saturday helping Grandfather in his garden. She would get hot and dirty, and when she was finished, her legs and back would ache. "Mother, please help me get out of this. My friends are going ice skating at the mall, and I really, really want to go with them."

"No, dear, you made this date with your grandfather weeks ago. He is very excited about your helping him. And guess what? You'll get to spend the day with your five-year-old cousin, Amanda." Miranda let out a deep sigh.

Grandfather and Amanda arrived in a *flurry*. "Amanda, Miranda, Miranda, Amanda," the child chattered on and on. "My name is like yours, and I am like you, too. You're my best friend, Miranda." The older girl could not keep from smiling. Grandfather hugged her. "Come on, Sugarbuttons. Get a move on. Shake a leg, Sweetcakes."

"Oh, Grandfather, you and your silly names," Miranda laughed.

When they got to the garden, most of the hard work had been done. The dirt had been plowed and raked. Miranda and Grandfather hammered stakes and stretched string to mark the rows. "Amanda-Apple-Dumpling, bring the measuring stick so we can space the rows evenly," he called.

Grandfather had brought juice and peanut butter crackers for a snack. "This is a picnic, and I just love picnics. Tell us a story, Gramps," Amanda said.

"Well, once there were Native Americans who lived here, Buttercup. They probably farmed this very field. They planted corn, beans, and squash. They called their three crops the Three Sisters, and they prayed for rain and sun to bring them a good harvest so they would have food for the winter. They planted in hills and put in four seeds and put a dead fish at the bottom."

"Yuck, why would anyone want to do that?" asked Amanda.

"I know," said Miranda. "As it rotted it made fertilizer for the plants."

"Right on, Honeybun," said Grandfather. "When I was a little boy, I helped my grandma plant her garden. We put four seeds in—one for the rabbit, one for the crow, one to rot, and one to grow."

"Will rabbits and birds eat our seeds?" asked Amanda, wide-eyed. The others nodded. "Then why don't we put in a whole bunch to be sure there are plenty for us?"

"Because, Kissyface, if the plants are too crowded, they won't be healthy. Each one needs room to grow," Grandfather explained.

Amanda stretched out on the blanket and was soon fast asleep. Miranda said, "Thanks, Gramps, for taking us out today. It's been fun."

GO

8 Miranda wanted to get out of helping Grandfather in order to —

    F plant her own garden.

    G do a baby-sitting job for pay.

    H go ice skating with her friends.

    J stay at home and study.

9 What lesson did Grandfather learn from his grandmother?

    A To plant extra seeds

    B To plant just one seed

    C To use fish for fertilizer

    D To chase rabbits away

10 In this story, the word *flurry* means —

    F sudden, brief gust of wind.

    G snowflakes blowing around.

    H with quick, hurried movements.

    J something done to confuse or bother.

11 What made Miranda smile first?

    A The heavy work in the garden had already been done.

    B Grandfather brought lunch.

    C Amanda told a funny story.

    D Amanda said Miranda was her best friend.

12 Which of these is true about Grandfather?

    F He sometimes forgot Amanda's name.

    G He used funny names for the children.

    H He went ice skating with Miranda.

    J He took a nap after gardening.

13 In order to keep the rows of plants straight, Grandfather asked Amanda to bring a —

    A shovel with marks.

    B folding ruler.

    C tape measure.

    D measuring stick.

14 Native Americans put a dead fish in each plant mound to —

    F make the soil fertile.

    G chase rabbits away.

    H signal when the crops were ready.

    J prevent seeds from rotting.

Example   **Directions:** Read each passage. Find the best answer to the questions that follow the passage.

In many parts of the United States, deer are becoming a problem. There are simply too many of them. When new housing developments are built on farmlands or near forests, the environment is improved for deer. They just love the lawns, plants, and flowers homeowners put in, which make for the perfect fast-food restaurant.

A Which of these is a problem for many suburban gardeners?

A Observing deer in the yard
B Finding plants that deer enjoy
C Keeping deer out of a garden
D Deer coming into the house

 Remember, some questions can't be answered by facts in the story. You have to "read between the lines" to find the answer.

Practice

Jane Goodall

Dr. Jane Goodall is known throughout the world as an expert on chimpanzees. She has spent many years studying these animals in the wilds of Africa and writing about them. Surprisingly, Dr. Goodall did not start her career as an animal behaviorist. She was fresh out of secretarial school and got a job with the famous paleontologist, Louis Leakey, who was studying prehistoric life forms. He sent her to Africa to study apes and chimps. Dr. Leakey hoped to find that ancient apes were the forebears of both chimps and humans. Jane Goodall did not find that connection at all, and her work took a different turn from what her mentor expected. Dr. Leakey encouraged Goodall to continue her work as a scientist, although it was in a field very different from his.

Goodall's motivation to study primates has been simply to learn about them, not to apply what she has learned to humans. Nonetheless, she has found that chimps and humans have many physical and behavioral similarities. Chimps can gesture to one another, and they seem to experience embarrassment and guilt.

Dr. Goodall would prefer to spend all her time in the jungle learning about chimps, but she makes frequent trips around the world to educate people about the difficult situation of the chimps. She hopes that her work will inspire others to study chimps and help these important animals survive. She feels that research in the field of studying chimp behavior has just begun, and hopes others will extend her work.

1   In addition to studying chimpanzees, Dr. Goodall is concerned about —

A   ancient humans.

B   saving the rainforest.

C   comparing chimps and humans.

D   their future.

2   There is enough information in this article to show that —

F   chimpanzees are nothing like humans.

G   scientists do not always find what they expect.

H   there is nothing left to be learned about chimps.

J   chimps are no longer in danger.

Read the poem and the questions. Choose the answer that is better than the others.

As the sun drops low in the west
And begins its journey that makes the night,
Its final rays make the eastern mountains blush,
The color of an open watermelon in July.

I pull the reins and slow the horse to a steady trot
Then turn and face the mountain, rich with color.
It fades to purple, then to darkness,
And the evening breeze cools the air.

I think about the wanderers of long ago
Who reached this spot so far from home.
"There is no better place," they must have said,
And felt my joy at the desert sunset.

3 An "open watermelon in July" is —

A one that is almost ripe.

B one that is delicious.

C an unusual one that has pink skin.

D one that has been cut open.

4 The narrator and the horse —

F had been riding slower.

G had been riding faster.

H had been herding cows.

J had been exploring the mountain.

5 The area in which the narrator is riding —

A is near a river.

B is on the eastern side of a mountain.

C is close to a large city.

D had been settled long ago.

6 In this poem, the "journey that makes the night" is —

F the time when the sun is below the horizon.

G the long trip the poet has yet to take.

H the trip made by wanderers of long ago.

J the time when the sun rises behind the mountain.

GO

The Supreme Law of the Land

After the Revolutionary War, the citizens of the newly formed United States thought their problems were over. They had defeated the most powerful nation in the world and now occupied a rich land. They discovered, however, that things were not as rosy as they seemed.

The governing body of the United States, the Continental Congress, was facing bankruptcy because it had no guaranteed source of revenue. In addition, armed mobs in Massachusetts were revolting against the state government, which had imposed heavy taxes and created harsh laws to punish those who owed money. The individual states were not working together well, which weakened the international trading position of the United States and affected its ability to defend itself.

A convention was called by the Continental Congress and several of the states in 1787. Taking place in Philadelphia, the Constitutional Convention was meant to create amendments to the existing Articles of Confederation, which were considered at the time to be America's Constitution. The Articles of Confederation were felt to be so weak, however, that those attending the convention decided to create a whole new constitution.

More than fifty delegates from 12 of the 13 states attended the convention. They included lawyers, farmers, merchants, and heroes of the Revolutionary War. George Washington presided over the meeting, which many historians feel created a brilliant document that has certainly withstood the test of time.

In the beginning of the convention, the delegates agreed on a three-part government that included the legislative, executive, and judicial branches. They disagreed considerably, however, on how the states would be represented in the legislature. The large population states wanted representation by population, while the small states wanted each state to be represented by the same number of legislators. A compromise was reached in which the legislature would have two houses, a Senate and a House of Representatives. Each state would have two senators, but the number of representatives would be determined by the population of the state. This compromise reflects the makeup of Congress today.

The difference of opinion regarding representation was not the only controversy that took place at the convention. Disputes also arose between delegates from manufacturing and agricultural states, who wanted the Constitution to favor their particular industry. Another disagreement was how the President, the chief of the executive branch of government, would be elected.

In spite of the disputes, a draft of the Constitution was completed, and on September 17 of 1787, it was signed by 39 of the 42 delegates. The matter now went to the individual states, who debated the Constitution and eventually agreed to it. The last state to ratify the Constitution was Rhode Island, which agreed to it on May 29 of 1790.

The Constitution is, in its own words, "the supreme law of the land." The first eight articles of the Constitution established the responsibilities of the various branches of government, how the President is elected, the relationship among the states, and how the Constitution itself can be amended. To these articles were quickly added ten amendments, which we know as the Bill of Rights. The Bill of Rights defines the most important rights of individuals and also delegates to the states any powers not held by the federal government. Since 1791, when the Bill of Rights was created, seventeen more amendments have been added to the Constitution.

The most remarkable thing about the Constitution and the Bill of Rights is that they are as important today as they were two hundred years ago. The first amendment, for example, guarantees citizens freedom to practice the religion of their choice, freedom of speech and the press, the right to gather together peaceably, and the opportunity to criticize the government without fear of *retaliation*. These guarantees were necessary in the 1700s because people were concerned that the new government of the United States would be as oppressive as the British government they had just defeated. Today, these same rights are exercised by Americans every day, who can attend the church of their choice, join political parties that disagree with government policies, or write a letter to the editor of a paper expressing an opinion about a mayor, governor, or the President.

7 **In the last paragraph, what does the word "retaliation" mean?**

A punishment

B payment

C privacy

D performance

8 **If a person is accused of a crime, that person is guaranteed a trial by a jury. This guarantee would probably be found in —**

F the first eight articles of the Constitution.

G the Constitutional Convention.

H the Bill of Rights.

J the last amendment.

9 **What was necessary before the Constitution could be enacted?**

A England had to agree to it.

B The states had to fight with one another.

C There had to be three branches of government.

D The states had to agree to it.

10 **The phrase "withstood the test of time" means the Constitution —**

F was created long ago.

G was written on durable paper.

H was signed by many mature people.

J has proven useful over many years.

11 **If there is a conflict between the laws of a state and the Constitution —**

A the state law is considered to be the higher law.

B the Constitution is considered to be the higher law.

C they are considered to be equal.

D both laws are considered to be invalid.

12 **Why did the large states want representation by population?**

F The greater a state's population, the fewer votes it would have.

G The greater a state's population, the more votes it would have.

H They wanted to give states equal power.

J They wanted people to move there.

GO >

Where are the cows?

Melissa woke with a start. Was it time to get up for school? No, it was still dark outside, and besides, summer vacation had started yesterday. She lay back on her comfortable bed. A soft breeze ruffled the curtains, and the smell of hay from the meadow drifted in. She sighed happily, but wondered what had awakened her?

As she stared at the ceiling, Melissa noticed the room become a little brighter. She looked out the window and saw a bright circle of lights slowly descend to the field next to the house. At first she thought it was a helicopter, but it made almost no noise at all. She was beginning to be afraid, but was fascinated by the lights. Melissa had no idea what this huge thing was, but it was much bigger than a school bus or the largest tractor she had ever seen.

Surprisingly, there was no movement or sound in the house. No one else had awakened, and the dog hadn't barked at all. In fact, everything was so quiet inside and outside the house that it was eerie.

Melissa looked out the window again, and the lights were gone. The cattle were snorting, and the dog was sniffing around the house. Crickets chirped, the wind blew the leaves, and all the normal night sounds had returned.

The next morning, Mother greeted her, "Well, sleepyhead, your sisters are already up enjoying vacation." Dad came in as she slumped over her cereal bowl. Now would be a good time to tell them. They wouldn't make fun of her and call her a "fraidy cat" the way her sisters would. Gina and Beth thought Melissa was the most fearful farm girl who had ever lived, and they teased her about it often.

Dad began talking. "I can't imagine what has been happening. That is the third cow that's been missing in two weeks. There are no tire prints or footprints. The fence wire wasn't cut. We haven't heard unusual noises. They've just disappeared. The sheriff told me there have been animals missing from several places around here."

Melissa gulped. She was sure the big circle of lights had been connected to the missing cows. UFO's only happened in the movies, she thought, not to perfectly normal families. She had dreamed it, she decided. Perhaps she was wise not to mention it. Just then her sisters came whooping into the house with a basket of baby ducks they had found in the barn. Melissa wasn't afraid of those and ran over to see them.

As the years passed, Melissa never forgot the bright lights. The mystery of the missing cows remained unsolved. But every time she read a story or saw a movie about aliens, Melissa thought of that summer night long ago and the circle of lights she saw.

GO

13 In which section of the library would a story like this most likely be found?

A History

B Mysteries

C Science

D Biography

14 There is enough information in the story to show that —

F some people believe in UFO's.

G Melissa dreamed the whole thing.

H Melissa was sad about the cows.

J people have long memories.

15 The last paragraph tells the reader —

A that Melissa told her family the story.

B that the missing cows were found.

C that Melissa was still frightened.

D that the mystery was never solved.

16 According to this passage, Melissa lived in —

F the city.

G the country.

H a foreign country.

J the suburbs.

17 In the first paragraph, *to wake with a start* means —

A to wake slowly.

B to fall back to sleep.

C to start dreaming.

D to wake quickly.

18 When her sisters brought the baby ducks in, Melissa —

F forgot about the lights for a while.

G told the story of the lights.

H remembered where the missing cows were.

J thought they would make fun of her story.

19 The boxes below show some events described in the article.

Melissa is awakened.	She becomes afraid.	
1	2	3

Which of these belongs in Box 3?

A The circle of lights descend.

B The cows are found.

C The dog was sniffing.

D The room becomes brighter.

Example Directions: Read the selection. Choose the answer you think is correct.

E1

All Norm and Sheila wanted to do was go biking. Unfortunately, it seemed they were never going to get started. They hadn't ridden more than half a mile when Norm's tire went flat. They fixed it and continued on their ride. Two miles later, Sheila's chain broke. She repaired the chain with a gizmo from her tool kit and they set off for a third time. Maybe this time they would really be on their way.

Which of these titles is most appropriate for this passage?

A "Two Bikers"

B "A Slow Start"

C "The First Flat"

D "Handy Tools"

Here is a story about a boy who had an unusual experience. Read the story and then do numbers 1 through 9 on pages 34 and 35.

No one believes me, and I can understand why. Here's what happened, and I swear it's the truth.

Aunt Tiki, my sister Lydia, and I were fishing in the Delaware River just north of Easton. We don't take our fishing very seriously, and spend most the time hanging out, eating lunch, and listening to Aunt Tiki tell us stories about the family.

On this particular day, a Saturday in May, I had wandered about half a mile up the river to a spot I loved. The river was wide here, and a bend just below me made it impossible for Lydia and Aunt Tiki to see me. This is an important detail, as you will see later.

I tied a lure on my line and cast out about twenty yards. I retrieved the lure slowly, and after a few feet, I hooked a fish. It was a bass, and I returned it to the water after I brought it in. I release almost all of my fish and use barbless hooks so they are not injured.

In the next half hour, I caught three more bass and was having a wonderful time. It's not often that I catch this many fish in such a short period of time, and I was beginning to believe I was becoming a bass master. My confidence rose, and I decided to walk out into the river a little farther.

My next cast was beautiful, one of the longest I had ever made, and took my lure into the deepest part of the river where the current was the strongest. I let it sink for a few seconds then started bringing it back. When I turned the handle of my reel, however, the lure wouldn't budge. It felt as if I had hooked the bottom.

I was trying to decide if I should walk closer to the lure and see if I could unhook it when something unusual happened. My line moved up river. I had hooked a fish, and it felt huge!

GO

The fish swam upstream so fast I thought I was going to run out of line. I decided to chase after it and began running. After a few steps, I caught my foot on a rock and went tumbling into the river. I held onto the rod, however, and even though I was soaked from head to toe, I got up and continued to battle the fish.

After about a hundred yards, the fish reached a deep pool and stopped swimming upstream. This gave me a chance to continue the battle, and I began playing the fish in the way I had read about in magazines. The battle lasted for about fifteen minutes, and eventually I brought the fish in. I was absolutely amazed. I didn't know what kind of fish it was, but it was almost three feet long!

Just then, I heard some clapping and turned around. A bunch of people were standing on the bank looking at me, shouting, waving, and whistling. They must have seen the whole thing. Being a ham, I took a bow, then picked up the fish to show it to them. They clapped even louder, and I felt like a really big deal.

I looked at the fish and saw how beautiful it was. At first, I thought about how good it would look hanging on my wall. The more I thought about it, the worse I felt. There was only one thing to do. I put the fish in the water, carefully removed the hook, and moved it back and forth slowly to make sure water was passing through its gills. After a moment, the fish swam away slowly, and as if to say it was all right, jumped into the air and landed with a great splash. I stared at the water for a few minutes and then headed back to shore.

In the crowd at the shore was an older gentleman who came up to me and asked to shake my hand. He said the fish was a salmon, which was extremely rare in the Delaware, and the one I had returned was a female loaded with eggs. If she could find a male, there was a chance that she would lay her eggs and that the young salmon would someday return to the river.

I ran back to Lydia and Aunt Tiki and told them the story. They didn't believe me. When I got back to school, I told all of my friends. They all said it was the best fish story they had ever heard, but none of them believed me. Well, it happened, and some day when we go back to the river, that kindly older gentleman will show up, and Lydia and Aunt Tiki will believe me.

The web on the right is based on the story. Use the web to do number 1.

1   Which of these phrases belongs in Circle 1?

A Describes landing the fish

B Builds suspense

C Makes fun of himself

D Tells about reaction of others

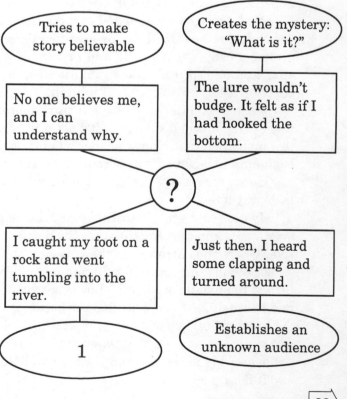

GO

2 Why does the author start out by insisting the story is true?

F The story is about fish.

G He doesn't know the reader.

H It is a fiction story.

J Nobody else believes him.

3 Why is it important to know that a bend in the river prevented Aunt Tiki and Lydia from seeing the author?

A Had they seen him, they would have believed him.

B The best fishing was around the bend in the river.

C The bend in the river brought the author closer to the deep part.

D The current was strongest above the bend in the river.

4 Which of these might make Aunt Tiki and Lydia believe the story?

F Reading about salmon and the Delaware

G Talking to a fishing expert

H Talking to someone who saw it

J Visiting the spot where it happened

5 In the fifth paragraph, what is a "bass master"?

A Someone who enjoys eating bass

B Someone who returns bass to the river

C Someone who is good at catching bass

D Someone who fishes for bass alone

6 What is the author's purpose in writing this passage?

F To explain how to catch large fish in unexpected places

G To show that Aunt Tiki and Lydia were wrong

H To help the reader understand the author's love of fishing

J To please the reader by sharing an unusual story

7 Why did the older gentleman want to shake the author's hand?

A He did the right thing by returning the fish to the river.

B He caught a large and unusual fish.

C No one would believe the author later when he told the story.

D The author put on a good show.

8 What does it mean to be a "ham"?

F To clap for people

G To catch large fish in unexpected places

H To enjoy a picnic more than fishing

J To put on a show in front of a crowd

9 What made the author sad?

A Knowing no one would believe him

B Thinking of killing the fish

C Tumbling into the river

D Knowing Aunt Tiki and Lydia hadn't seen his fish

GO

ANSWER ROWS   2 Ⓕ Ⓖ Ⓗ Ⓙ   4 Ⓕ Ⓖ Ⓗ Ⓙ   6 Ⓕ Ⓖ Ⓗ Ⓙ   8 Ⓕ Ⓖ Ⓗ Ⓙ
                     3 Ⓐ Ⓑ Ⓒ Ⓓ   5 Ⓐ Ⓑ Ⓒ Ⓓ   7 Ⓐ Ⓑ Ⓒ Ⓓ   9 Ⓐ Ⓑ Ⓒ Ⓓ

We Don't Want to Move

Stan didn't want to move. He was happy with the house they lived in, the school he attended, and the friends he had known for so long. He didn't understand why they had to pack up and move 2000 miles to Montana.

"I know you aren't happy about this," Mrs. Howard said, "but we don't have any choice in the matter. My company wants me to take over a new division, and I'd like to give it a try. It's a good career move, and I'll be paid a lot more."

"What about Dad's job? What about school for me and Nan? Haven't you thought about the rest of us?"

"Of course I have. Your father loves the idea of moving. We've saved a little money and have decided to buy a small business there. He's always wanted to be his own boss, and this is a chance for him to give it a try. The schools where we are moving have a great reputation, and I'm sure you and Nan will make new friends. Besides, they have telephones in Montana, so you'll be able to call your old friends. We're not moving to another planet."

In his heart, Stan knew his mother was right, but he still didn't like it. Montana was nowhere, and he was certain the kids there would be geeks. What on earth would he do there? One of his friends told him that the nearest mall would be a thousand miles away! He didn't believe this, of course, but he was concerned that he'd be bored to tears.

Just then, Nan came through the front door with the day's mail. She was just as unhappy about the move as Stan was. She dropped the mail on the table and sat down beside Stan. Both of them had long faces.

"Here's something you can look at."

Mrs. Howard handed them a thick envelope. It was from the Bozeman Chamber of Commerce, the town they were moving to. Nan opened it and began thumbing through the flyers. One was about schools, another was about businesses...nothing of interest to her or her brother. Then Nan's eye caught another brochure with the title *Fun in Big Sky Country*.

"Look at this, Stan. People actually have fun in Montana."

"Yeah, right. What do they do, watch the rocks get old?"

"Well, there are two ski areas right near town. One is Bridger Bowl and the other is Big Sky. Have you ever heard of them?"

"You're kidding! They're world class. Let me see that."

Sure enough, the two ski areas were less than an hour from town. So was great fishing, hiking, and mountain biking. Yellowstone National Park was just a few hours away, and there were more national forests than you could explore in a lifetime.

"Why didn't you and dad tell us about all this stuff? I mean, this is great. There are a zillion things to do in Montana."

"We tried, but you two were being such grumps that we decided to let you find out on your own. So, you think you'll be able to tolerate the move?"

GO

10 Who said, "People actually have fun in Montana."?

F Nan

G Stan

H Mrs. Howard

J You can't tell from the story.

11 The statement "the nearest mall would be a thousand miles away" is —

A an example of simile.

B an example of metaphor.

C an accurate description.

D an exaggeration.

12 The expression "Both of them had long faces" means the two children —

F were angry.

G looked alike.

H were unhappy.

J liked where they lived.

13 Which of these is another good title for this story?

A "A Change of Heart"

B "Things to Do in Montana"

C "Making New Friends"

D "A Better Job"

14 According to a dictionary, someone is "inconsiderate" if they *lack regard for the feelings of others*. Which of these is an example of being inconsiderate?

F The children changing their mind about the move

G The children not wanting to move to Montana

H The children's mother being promoted to a better job

J The children's father wanting to be his own boss

15 Which of these best describes the children at the end of the story?

A Surprised

B Disappointed

C Concerned

D Isolated

16 The answer you chose for number 15 is best because the story shows that —

F the children's mother received more money for the new job.

G schools in Montana were better than the children's current school.

H the children's father didn't mind giving up his current job.

J the children discovered Montana was more interesting than they thought.

GO >

MEMORANDUM

From: Principal Jones
To: Students and Teachers
Concerning: School Play Day next Monday

On Monday, all classes will be dismissed at 10:15 AM, and the school will have a spring play day. Homeroom teachers will have sign-up sheets for the various activities all this week. Lunch and soft drink passes will be distributed just before the dismissal on Monday. The following is a tentative schedule of events.

10:15-11:00   Softball game, 8th grade boys vs. 7th grade boys, north ball field; Contest—girls' basketball free throws, gymnasium; horseshoe tournament, all students, south playground

11:00-11:30   Students with A Lunch passes eat
11:30-12:00   Students with B Lunch passes eat
12:00-12:30   Students with C Lunch passes eat

11:00-12:30   Music, south playground; contest—boys' basketball free throws, gymnasium

12:30- 1:30   Three-legged race; sack race; croquet tournament (all on south playground)

1:30- 2:00   Soft drinks in the concession area

1:30- 2:30   Girls' volleyball tournament; boys' volleyball tournament (both on north ball field)

2:30- 3:30   Pep rally with band and cheerleaders; classes' cheering contest; announcement of winners in all events; presentation of ribbons and medals (gymnasium)

Food and prizes have been donated by the following merchants:

Ubuildit Lumber Yard	Festival Food Store
The Happy Hamburger	Athletic Apparel
Toys for the World	Busy Bee Flower
and Gift Shop	

GO

17 Which of these events is not on the schedule?

A Volleyball for boys

B Three-legged races

C Basketball free throw for boys

D Softball for girls

18 What will the students do before 10:15 AM?

F They will be in class.

G They will line up for the opening parade.

H They will not arrive at school until 10:15.

J They will sit in the gym and talk with their friends.

19 Who provided money for the food and prizes?

A The principal

B Local merchants

C The school

D The students

20 This memo would probably be —

F published in the local newspaper.

G displayed on the local cable television station.

H distributed to the teachers and read to the students.

J presented to the school board for approval.

21 What can students do while they are eating lunch?

A Listen to music

B Play volleyball

C Watch the girls shoot baskets in the gym

D Leave the campus for the awards

22 Which of these does *not* take place on the south playground?

F Croquet tournament

G Girl's volleyball tournament

H Horseshoe tournament

J Three-legged race

GO

Leadbelly

When young people today slip a CD into a player and listen to their favorite musician, they probably don't realize that they are enjoying the legacy of "Leadbelly." Born in 1888 in Louisiana, Huddie Ledbetter was a blues guitarist who inspired generations of musicians. Much of his work has been saved in the Library of Congress, and he is generally considered to be one of our national treasures.

As a child, Leadbelly learned to play several instruments. His favorite instrument was the 12-string guitar, which eventually made him famous. Leadbelly's playing had a unique sound that many musicians tried to imitate, but no one was able to duplicate it.

For much of Huddie Ledbetter's adult life, he wandered from place to place, playing anywhere he could and sometimes getting into trouble with the law. In 1934, he was discovered by John and Alan Lomax, who helped Leadbelly find a larger audience for his music. He was soon playing in colleges, clubs, and music halls around the country. Leadbelly was featured on radio and television shows, gave concerts in New York's Town Hall, and performed in Europe.

Leadbelly died in 1949, but his music lives on. Musicians in every style credit him with laying the foundation for today's popular music. From rock and roll to rap, Leadbelly is truly one of the roots of American music.

23   What was the turning point in Leadbelly's life?

A   Learning to play music as a young boy

B   Being imitated by other musicians

C   Being discovered by the Lomax brothers

D   Appearing on television and radio shows

24   How did Leadbelly probably get his nickname?

F   Leadbelly sounds like Ledbetter.

G   His guitar had lead strings.

H   He led an interesting life.

J   He was probably overweight.

25   In the second paragraph, what does the word "unique" mean?

A   Similar to everyone else's

B   Meant for people from the South

C   Meant for large concert halls

D   Different from everyone else's

26   Which of these statements is supported by the text?

F   The "blues" is a form of music that is no longer played.

G   Leadbelly influenced many musicians, including some alive today.

H   When Huddie Ledbetter was discovered, he was already famous.

J   American music was discovered by Huddie Ledbetter.

27   This article is mostly about —

A   how to become a famous musician.

B   two brothers who discovered the blues.

C   a talented but little-known musician.

D   the roots of today's music.

GO

For Numbers 28 through 31, choose the best answer to the question.

28 Did you every wonder why bears don't have tails? Long ago, they did, but they lost them. Here's how it happened.

A paragraph like this would most likely be found in a book of —

F fables.

G facts.

H science fiction stories.

J adventure stories.

29 **Which of these sentences probably came from a science fiction story?**

A The eagle sat on a branch high in a dead tree and watched the lake for signs of fish near the surface.

B The crew on the ship was becoming restless after two months of sailing without any sign of land ahead.

C One by one, the stars began winking out, and the night sky slowly became a sea of unbroken blackness.

D The disastrous flood left thousands of people homeless, but led to the redevelopment of the area.

30 **Which of these statements makes use of a simile?**

F It was a lazy day, hot and humid, without even a breeze.

G Clouds rolled in from the west and darkened the sky.

H The sound of thunder scattered the birds like leaves before the wind.

J Torrents of rain fell suddenly, soaking everyone in the park.

31 The math test was just two days away, and Chuck's stomach was in knots. Every time he started to study, something happened to prevent him from getting down to work. He had to do something or he'd never pass.

Which of these best explains the meaning of the phrase "his stomach was in knots"?

A Chuck was annoyed that he hadn't studied.

B Chuck felt nervous because he wasn't ready for the test.

C Chuck really didn't care how he did on the math test.

D Everything seemed to bother Chuck these days.

STOP

To the Student:

These tests will give you a chance to put the tips you have learned to work.

A few last reminders…

- Be sure you understand all the directions before you begin each test. You may ask the teacher questions about the directions if you do not understand them.
- Work as quickly as you can during each test.
- When you change an answer, be sure to erase your first mark completely.

- You can guess at an answer or skip difficult items and go back to them later.
- Use the tips you have learned whenever you can.
- It is OK to be a little nervous. You may even do better.

Now that you have completed the lessons in this unit, you are on your way to scoring high!

STUDENT'S NAME		SCHOOL
LAST / FIRST / MI		TEACHER

FEMALE ◯   MALE ◯

BIRTH DATE

MONTH	DAY	YEAR
JAN	0 0	0
FEB	1 1	1
MAR	2 2	2
APR	3 3	3
MAY	4	4
JUN	5	5 5
JUL	6	6 6
AUG	7	7 7
SEP	8	8 8
OCT	9	9 9
NOV		
DEC		

GRADE

⑥   ⑦   ⑧

PART 1   VOCABULARY

E1 Ⓐ Ⓑ Ⓒ Ⓓ	6 Ⓕ Ⓖ Ⓗ Ⓙ	13 Ⓐ Ⓑ Ⓒ Ⓓ	20 Ⓕ Ⓖ Ⓗ Ⓙ	27 Ⓐ Ⓑ Ⓒ Ⓓ	31 Ⓐ Ⓑ Ⓒ Ⓓ
E2 Ⓕ Ⓖ Ⓗ Ⓙ	7 Ⓐ Ⓑ Ⓒ Ⓓ	14 Ⓕ Ⓖ Ⓗ Ⓙ	21 Ⓐ Ⓑ Ⓒ Ⓓ	28 Ⓕ Ⓖ Ⓗ Ⓙ	32 Ⓕ Ⓖ Ⓗ Ⓙ
1 Ⓐ Ⓑ Ⓒ Ⓓ	8 Ⓕ Ⓖ Ⓗ Ⓙ	15 Ⓐ Ⓑ Ⓒ Ⓓ	22 Ⓕ Ⓖ Ⓗ Ⓙ	29 Ⓐ Ⓑ Ⓒ Ⓓ	33 Ⓐ Ⓑ Ⓒ Ⓓ
2 Ⓕ Ⓖ Ⓗ Ⓙ	9 Ⓐ Ⓑ Ⓒ Ⓓ	16 Ⓕ Ⓖ Ⓗ Ⓙ	23 Ⓐ Ⓑ Ⓒ Ⓓ	30 Ⓕ Ⓖ Ⓗ Ⓙ	34 Ⓕ Ⓖ Ⓗ Ⓙ
3 Ⓐ Ⓑ Ⓒ Ⓓ	10 Ⓕ Ⓖ Ⓗ Ⓙ	17 Ⓐ Ⓑ Ⓒ Ⓓ	24 Ⓕ Ⓖ Ⓗ Ⓙ		
4 Ⓕ Ⓖ Ⓗ Ⓙ	11 Ⓐ Ⓑ Ⓒ Ⓓ	18 Ⓕ Ⓖ Ⓗ Ⓙ	25 Ⓐ Ⓑ Ⓒ Ⓓ		
5 Ⓐ Ⓑ Ⓒ Ⓓ	12 Ⓕ Ⓖ Ⓗ Ⓙ	19 Ⓐ Ⓑ Ⓒ Ⓓ	26 Ⓕ Ⓖ Ⓗ Ⓙ		

PART 2   READING COMPREHENSION

E1 Ⓐ Ⓑ Ⓒ Ⓓ	6 Ⓕ Ⓖ Ⓗ Ⓙ	12 Ⓕ Ⓖ Ⓗ Ⓙ	18 Ⓕ Ⓖ Ⓗ Ⓙ	24 Ⓕ Ⓖ Ⓗ Ⓙ	30 Ⓕ Ⓖ Ⓗ Ⓙ
1 Ⓐ Ⓑ Ⓒ Ⓓ	7 Ⓐ Ⓑ Ⓒ Ⓓ	13 Ⓐ Ⓑ Ⓒ Ⓓ	19 Ⓐ Ⓑ Ⓒ Ⓓ	25 Ⓐ Ⓑ Ⓒ Ⓓ	31 Ⓐ Ⓑ Ⓒ Ⓓ
2 Ⓕ Ⓖ Ⓗ Ⓙ	8 Ⓕ Ⓖ Ⓗ Ⓙ	14 Ⓕ Ⓖ Ⓗ Ⓙ	20 Ⓕ Ⓖ Ⓗ Ⓙ	26 Ⓕ Ⓖ Ⓗ Ⓙ	32 Ⓕ Ⓖ Ⓗ Ⓙ
3 Ⓐ Ⓑ Ⓒ Ⓓ	9 Ⓐ Ⓑ Ⓒ Ⓓ	15 Ⓐ Ⓑ Ⓒ Ⓓ	21 Ⓐ Ⓑ Ⓒ Ⓓ	27 Ⓐ Ⓑ Ⓒ Ⓓ	33 Ⓐ Ⓑ Ⓒ Ⓓ
4 Ⓕ Ⓖ Ⓗ Ⓙ	10 Ⓕ Ⓖ Ⓗ Ⓙ	16 Ⓕ Ⓖ Ⓗ Ⓙ	22 Ⓕ Ⓖ Ⓗ Ⓙ	28 Ⓕ Ⓖ Ⓗ Ⓙ	34 Ⓕ Ⓖ Ⓗ Ⓙ
5 Ⓐ Ⓑ Ⓒ Ⓓ	11 Ⓐ Ⓑ Ⓒ Ⓓ	17 Ⓐ Ⓑ Ⓒ Ⓓ	23 Ⓐ Ⓑ Ⓒ Ⓓ	29 Ⓐ Ⓑ Ⓒ Ⓓ	

Part 1   Vocabulary

Examples   **Directions:** For E1, mark the answer that has almost the same meaning as the underlined word. For E2, read the question. Mark the answer you think is correct.

E1 durable cloth

   A strong
   B pretty
   C flimsy
   D woven

E2 Which of these probably comes from the Latin word *solitarius* meaning *alone*?

   F soldier
   G solid
   H solitary
   J solar

For numbers 1-8, find the word or words that mean the same or almost the same as the underlined word.

1   recently employed

   A long
   B lonely
   C unlikely
   D newly

5   Listless means about the same as —

   A enthusiastic
   B harmless
   C livid
   D uninterested

2   mended shoes

   F fashionable
   G repaired
   H expensive
   J attractive

6   Abundant means about the same as —

   F little
   G confused
   H much
   J limited

3   nomadic tribe

   A large
   B primitive
   C wandering
   D peaceful

7   To ensnare is to —

   A trap
   B relinquish
   C seek
   D release

4   vague plans

   F complicated
   G unclear
   H exciting
   J understandable

8   A passage is a kind of —

   F river
   G route
   H vacation
   J train

GO

9 A **faulty** switch caused the blackout.

If something is faulty it is —

A inexpensive
B defective
C powerful
D loose

10 Did you **request** that room?

To request is to —

F visit
G pay for
H enjoy
J ask for

11 Larinna doesn't make **hasty** decisions.

Hasty means —

A difficult
B important
C quick
D unpleasant

12 Put the equipment on the **platform**.

A platform is a —

F table
G kind of stage
H waterproof carpet
J truck

13 Alan enjoyed the **solitude** of the beach.

Solitude means —

A being with others
B crowded place
C high mountain
D being alone

For numbers 14-19, find the word that means the opposite of the underlined word.

14 an **exciting** journey

F long
G thrilling
H uneventful
J awesome

15 **odd** behavior

A normal
B strange
C aggressive
D unkind

16 **propose** an idea

F suggest
G criticize
H withdraw
J analyze

17 **inform** his friends

A keep information from
B avoid
C give information to
D join

18 **outwit** an opponent —

F be stronger than
G be less clever than
H be faster than
J be more clever than

19 **jovial** uncle —

A unhappy
B general
C horrible
D remarkable

GO

For numbers 20-23, choose the word that correctly completes <u>both</u> sentences.

20 Woody will _____ the winning ticket from a hat.

What did you _____ in art class?

F pick
G draw
H paint
J choose

21 Did you _____ your homework?

The water damaged the _____ of the desk.

A complete
B finish
C surface
D appearance

22 What made that _____ ?

The house has a _____ roof.

F sound
G strong
H noise
J sloped

23 Put the chair in that _____ .

They tried to _____ the silver market.

A room
B control
C corner
D position

24 | She earned a <u>degree</u> in biology. |

In which sentence does the word degree mean the same thing as in the sentence above?

F The temperature rose just one <u>degree</u> all day.

G To what <u>degree</u> did the vacation affect your school work?

H Only a slight <u>degree</u> of difference existed between the two choices.

J A college <u>degree</u> will allow you to make a better living.

25 | The seventh <u>grade</u> class took a trip. |

In which sentence does the word <u>grade</u> mean the same thing as in the sentence above?

A Heavy equipment was used to <u>grade</u> the rocky road.

B The teacher will <u>grade</u> the papers over the weekend.

C Each <u>grade</u> in this school shares the same team of teachers.

D What <u>grade</u> did you earn on the test?

26 | Which <u>button</u> starts the machine? |

In which sentence does the word <u>button</u> mean the same thing as in the sentence above?

F A <u>button</u> on my coat popped off.

G She took aim and hit the target right on the <u>button</u>.

H The <u>button</u> on the elevator lights up when you press it.

J <u>Button</u> your coat before you go out into the cold.

GO

27 Which of these words probably comes from the German word *eitel* meaning *inactive*?

A either
B island
C title
D idle

28 Which of these words probably comes from the Latin word *mutuus* meaning *interchanged*?

F municipal
G multiply
H mutual
J mutter

29 A _____ light filled the sky.

Which of these words means the light was very bright?

A brilliant
B colorful
C mysterious
D potential

30 The pond was _____ as the sun set behind the mountain.

Which of these words means the pond was peaceful and quiet?

F notable
G evasive
H serene
J regenerated

Read the paragraph. Find the word below the paragraph that fits best in each numbered blank.

Big changes are underway in, of all things, television. Within the next five years, many ___(31)___ of this familiar home appliance will change dramatically. The changes will affect how signals are received, the ___(32)___ of the picture, and the content of programming.

Today, most television sets receive signals through the airwaves or dedicated cables. Soon, however, these signals will be ___(33)___ over the same cables that carry your telephone service. In addition, the signal will be ___(34)___ significantly so the picture will have the same quality as that shown in a movie theater.

31 A purchase
B aspects
C support
D decorate

32 F quality
G recently
H probably
J abruptly

33 A fill
B drill
C mine
D transmitted

34 F record
G cost
H enhanced
J rely

47

STOP

Example   Directions: Read the selection. Mark the answer you think is correct.

E1 Fashions come and go, but sweats seem to last forever. Thirty years ago, sweats came in one color—gray—and one style—baggy. Today, however, sweats come in every color you can imagine and in a broad range of styles. Parents dress toddlers in sweats, and senior citizens find them to be the perfect outfit for everyday activities. The biggest market for sweats, however, is teenagers and young adults.	**A The largest market for sweats is —** **A** teenagers and young adults. **B** parents and toddlers. **C** senior citizens. **D** athletes.

Here is a passage about ways you can invest for your future. Read the story and then do numbers 1 through 7 on page 49.

Ben Franklin once said that, "A penny saved is a penny earned." In today's world, however, it's not enough to just save. If you really want to get ahead, you must invest.

Investing is the practice of using money to make money. Typically, people invest their surplus funds that are not needed for basics such as food, housing, clothing, taxes, and the like. Investing provides businesses with the money or capital they need to grow, to provide jobs, and to offer you a wide variety of products and services.

Many options are available for people who have money to invest. One of the safest and most popular investments is the certificate of deposit, which is available through most banks. When you invest in a certificate of deposit or CD, you promise to leave a certain amount of money in the bank for a specified period of time. During that period of time, you earn interest on your CD. For example, if you bought a CD for $1000 and promised to leave it in the bank for a year, you might earn 5 percent interest or $50.

A bond is another popular investment. When you buy a bond, you are, in fact, lending money to a company or the federal government. The institution issuing the bond promises to repay you for the principal you lent them plus a specified amount of interest. Let's say you bought a $1000 bond issued by General Motors, a company that makes automobiles. The company might promise to pay you 6% interest each year and then return your $1000 in the year 2010.

A third type of investment is common stock. When you buy stock in a company, you become one of the owners of the company. Suppose you bought 100 shares of XYZ company at $10 each. That would mean you own $1000 worth of that company. If the company is successful, it will earn money and your part of the company will be worth more than the $1000 you paid for it.

In addition, some companies pay a dividend, which is like interest. From the earnings of the XYZ Company, the board of directors might pay each shareholder an annual dividend of 3%. Your $1000 in stock would earn you $30 a year.

Different investments have different levels of risk. CDs have almost no risk at all. They are insured by the federal government so your investment is safe. Bonds are somewhat riskier because a company can fail and not be able to either pay you interest or return your principal. It is rare when a company fails in this way, so bonds are considered to be only moderately risky.

Buying stock is usually the riskiest of the three investments we've discussed, chiefly because companies might not be as successful as you or the management hopes. If a company fails, you might lose your whole investment. It is also possible that the company could do much better than anyone anticipated. When this happens, your $1000 might double or even triple in a few years.

GO

1 **According to this passage, money that is invested is used to —**

A buy products.

B pay for services.

C help businesses grow.

D pay for infrastructure.

2 **When you buy stocks, you —**

F become a part owner of a company.

G earn interest.

H assume no risk.

J are insured by the federal government.

3 **Suppose you wanted to recommend a very safe investment to an older person who wanted to take no risks with their money. Which of these would you choose?**

A A bond

B A certificate of deposit

C Stock in a new company

D Stock in an established company

4 **This passage probably was written to —**

F encourage the reader to buy stocks.

G show how risky stocks are.

H show how bonds and CDs are better investments than are stocks.

J explain the differences among various investments.

5 **Which of these conclusions can be drawn from the passage?**

A Bonds are safer than CDs.

B The more risk you are willing to take, the more your investments might make.

C The less risk you are willing to take, the more your investments will make.

D Investing is only for rich people.

6 **Choose the sentence that best describes what the passage is mostly about.**

F It's always a good idea to save some of the money you earn.

G Most people worry that they don't have enough money.

H If you have money to invest, there are several possibilities available to you.

J A good job will let you earn extra money you can invest.

7 **In this passage, you learn that people with money to invest have several "options." The word *options* refers to —**

A choices.

B types of stock.

C extra money.

D interest.

Garlic, the Herb of Many Uses

Most people are familiar with garlic as a seasoning for cooking. Its pungent flavor is found in many dishes such as spaghetti, pizza, pot roasts, stews, salads, and breads. It is so popular that there are a number of books devoted completely to cooking with garlic.

But did you know that garlic is healthful, too, and has many other uses? Medical research has shown that eating garlic regularly can lower a person's blood pressure. Garlic sprays have been found to be as effective as chemicals in controlling insects such as mosquitoes. You might also be amazed to learn that some people even believe that a necklace of garlic will keep away vampires!

Many people love the flavor of garlic in foods, especially ethnic foods from Mexico, Italy, Eastern Europe, and China. Some gourmets like roasted garlic by itself, and a surprising number of people like to munch it raw. Because it is so pungent, garlic lovers worry that the smell of their favorite herb will linger on their breath. These people find that chewing the leaves of fresh parsley or basil will prevent garlic breath.

An *organic* insecticide spray can be made by liquefying garlic in a blender and combining it with water. Pepper can be added to the mixture to make it even more powerful. Because the mixture is harmless, it can be sprayed in the air, on places where insects are found, or even directly on plants to keep down garden pests. Garlic

also controls fungus, and some people claim the mixture kills fire ants when poured on their mounds. Planting garlic among ornamental and food plants in a garden seems to repel insects.

Because so many people believe garlic has important health benefits, health food stores sell garlic tablets and extract. People can use these if they don't want to put garlic on their food. True garlic lovers, however, will have none of this, and simply add garlic to as many foods as they can.

8 To make a garlic spray, it is first necessary to —

F mix pepper with garlic.

G liquefy garlic.

H use parsley leaves.

J choose an insecticide.

9 This passage would most likely be found in —

A a magazine about new kinds of chemicals and medicines.

B a journal for people who design gardens and orchards.

C a book about protecting a garden from insect pests.

D the gardening and cooking page of a newspaper.

10 People who want the benefits of garlic but who don't like the taste or smell of it can —

F take garlic tablets.

G liquefy garlic and water in the blender.

H avoid garlic altogether.

J plant garlic near other vegetables.

11 The purpose of this passage is to —

A convince people that garlic is the most useful herb.

B show that many foods can offer medical benefits.

C provide information about the many uses of a popular herb.

D introduce people to a new food product that is inexpensive.

12 What is the chief health benefit of garlic?

F Improved circulation

G Preventing insect bites

H Improved breathing

J Lower blood pressure

13 This passage would lead the reader to believe that one reason garlic spray works against insects is its —

A popularity.

B smell.

C health benefits.

D liquefaction.

14 You can tell from this passage that the word *organic* has to do with —

F being artificial.

G being natural.

H having a strong odor.

J being poisonous.

15 There is enough information in this passage to show that —

A chemical sprays are not as effective as natural products.

B people who believe in vampires cook often with garlic.

C common things can have more than one use.

D cooking with garlic makes food taste better than with other herbs.

GO

Surprising Summer

It was Maria's worst nightmare. Her mother was going to work in South America for July and August, and she was going to stay with her aunt and uncle in Utah. She loved Aunt Regina, Uncle Louis, and her cousins, Lillian and Zack, but as far as Maria was concerned, Utah was at the end of the earth. She was born and raised in Chicago, and she loved the excitement of the city, especially in the summer. Maria had convinced herself that this would be the worst summer of her life.

The flight from Chicago to Salt Lake City, Maria's first, was uneventful. She spent most of it reading and sleeping, and even discovered that airplane food was not as bad as she had expected. Every once in a while she looked out the window, however, and her fears were confirmed. The farther the plane got from Chicago, the fewer signs of civilization she saw. The landscape below was mostly hills, plains, deserts, and mountains. The only cities she saw were tiny, and their number got smaller as the plane got closer to Salt Lake City.

While the plane was circling before landing in Salt Lake City, Maria saw that the city was large, although much smaller than Chicago. A huge lake was nearby, just like Chicago, and incredible mountains were on the east. "It's pretty neat," she thought to herself, "but it isn't the Windy City."

Uncle Louis and Aunt Regina met Maria as she came out of the jetway. As they walked to the baggage area, Aunt Regina explained that Lillian and Zack were back at the hotel waiting for them. They were all going to spend the night in the city rather than trying to make the long drive to St. George in the southern part of the state.

By the time they had picked up the luggage and driven to the hotel, it was late in the afternoon. They decided to go out to dinner, and then the kids would go to a concert at the Delta Center. Maria was surprised because the group that was playing was one that was scheduled to perform in Chicago in a few weeks.

The next morning, as they headed south toward St. George, Maria, Lillian, and Zack slept in the back seat of the car. Whenever they woke up, they talked about the great time they had enjoyed the night before. After dinner, they had gone to a mall for an hour before the concert. After the concert, they went to a party with some other kids Lillian and Zack knew. They had been able to get around easily by bus and arrived back at the hotel just before midnight, as they had promised. Maria hated to admit it, but the night was just as much fun as she would have had in Chicago.

The ride to St. George was through beautiful country. Maria was amazed at how far she could see. In Chicago, the tall buildings prevented any great views, although you could always go to the lake and see for miles. Here, however, there were vistas in every direction, with mountains and mesas breaking up the desert landscape. Even the colors were unusual, with lots of reds, browns, and tans, but not many greens.

When they were almost to St. George, Zack started giggling and said, "Can we tell her now, Mom? I'm ready to explode."

"Okay," said Aunt Regina. "Maria, we're not going home quite yet. There's a huge lake nearby, Lake Powell, and we've rented a houseboat for a few days. It's a lot of fun, and we're sure you're going to like it."

Maria didn't quite know what to say. It sounded wonderful, and she had already had such a good time. Maybe this summer wouldn't be so bad after all. In fact, maybe this would be one of the best summers ever.

GO

16 **In the second paragraph, what does the word "uneventful" mean?**

F Without any unusual happenings

G Without a meal

H Without enjoyment

J Without anyone knowing her

17 **The story implies that —**

A Maria had been to Utah often before.

B Maria's mother would meet her in Utah.

C the weather is hot in Chicago in the summer.

D this was Maria's first airplane flight.

18 **Why did Zack say "I'm ready to explode"?**

F He had eaten too much.

G It was hot in the back of the car.

H He was having a hard time keeping a secret.

J He was angry because of the long car ride.

19 **How does the author set the tone in the first paragraph?**

A By making Maria seem like an unhappy person

B By making the job Maria's mother has sound exciting

C By making the reader think Maria will be unhappy in Utah

D By making the reader think Chicago is a great place to be in the summer

20 **It is clear from the story that —**

F Maria was bored on her first night in Salt Lake City.

G Maria's aunt and uncle have done a lot to make her feel happy.

H Maria's cousins are jealous because of all the attention she is receiving.

J Maria didn't mind leaving Chicago for the summer.

21 **In what way are Chicago and Salt Lake City alike?**

A Both cities are about the same size.

B Maria has cousins in both cities.

C Both cities are near a large lake.

D Mountains are near both cities.

22 **The three children in this story —**

F had never met before.

G were not very responsible.

H stayed out too late on the first night.

J are about the same age.

23 **Which of these changes occurs in the story?**

A Maria comes to dislike Chicago.

B Maria's attitude toward Utah improves.

C Maria decides she wants to live in Utah.

D Maria's cousins learn to appreciate her.

Free Movie Tickets

Students in Lowry public schools can earn free movie passes by doing community service work this summer. City Manager Tom Turner announced the special program and added that, "We have outstanding young people in this city who will help others if they have the chance. This is a way to encourage them and reward them for their work."

Projects are available for every age group, kindergarten through twelfth grade, and students may propose their own projects. Students may work with adult sponsors of their groups or with adult community volunteers. The sponsors must be registered with the city, and they will fill out forms verifying service hours worked. Free passes to the Lowry Cinema may be used for any showing this summer.

Passes will be issued as soon as a project has been completed, and there is no limit to the number of movie passes any individual can earn. The number of hours of work needed to earn a pass must be negotiated between the adult sponsor or supervisor and the city manager's office, and will depend on the difficulty of the work and the age of the student. Groups or individuals other than students can participate as volunteers in the project, but free movie passes will only be given to students.

The projects that the city is hoping will be done by the students include cleaning up vacant lots, planting flowers in parks and downtown areas, mowing and weeding public areas, and working at the recycling center. The Habitat for Humanity home building project is also a possibility for older students with some carpentry skills or a willingness to learn them. In the past, Habitat has built several homes for families that qualified for their assistance.

The public library has several storerooms that need to be cleaned and organized. Librarian Jane Brooks hopes to have enough volunteers to be able to hold an excess book sale in August to raise funds for the library's video section.

The city swimming pool can use additional clean-up crews from 7:00 until 9:00 weekday mornings to assist the employees, if volunteers want to work those hours. The abandoned railroad station downtown is in need of cleaning and repairs, although some sections need major repairs.

City Manager Turner and his staff are still collecting suggestions for projects for student participation. For more information, interested parties may contact Mrs. Sally Stapleton of the city manager's office at 555-5656 or drop by City Hall during normal business hours.

GO

24 **There is enough information in this announcement to show that the town —**

F wants students to go to the movies.

G has plenty of projects for students to do.

H has plenty of money to hire workers.

J wants to support the local movie theater.

25 **All of these people may earn free movie passes by doing community service work except—**

A children from out of town visiting relatives.

B high school students who work on the Habitat for Humanity house.

C seventh graders who help clean the swimming pool early in the morning.

D kindergarten students who plant flowers in the park.

26 **This announcement indicates that —**

F tickets are earned when a project is started.

G only one ticket per student can be earned.

H projects must be completed to earn tickets.

J one hour's work earns one ticket.

27 **The announcement tries to appeal to the students'—**

A need to earn money at jobs.

B desire to learn job skills.

C need to find something to do.

D desire to help their community.

28 **The announcement suggests that —**

F students can come up with their own projects.

G each project has a time limit.

H adult sponsors can earn movie tickets.

J city workers must supervise the students' projects.

29 **Which of these is an opinion in the announcement?**

A Mr. Turner thinks the town's students are outstanding.

B The town of Lowry has a variety of projects students can do.

C Adult supervisors will be sure everyone gets credit for his work.

D Students will work only if they are rewarded for it.

30 **The announcement was written mainly to tell about—**

F the different kinds of needs in the community.

G work being done by the city manager's staff.

H a book sale coming up to benefit the library.

J community service projects that reward students.

GO

For numbers 31 through 34, choose the best answer to the question.

31 His heart was in his throat as Larry stepped to the foul line with just seconds left in the game.

Which of these best explains the meaning of the phrase "his heart was in this throat"?

A   Larry was nervous.

B   Larry felt sick.

C   Larry had been injured.

D   Larry felt confident.

32 **Which of these sentences probably came from an adventure story?**

F   Mountain ranges are formed when sections of the earth's crust are pushed together.

G   Young Nate looked at the snow-covered peaks they would somehow have to cross before reaching Oregon.

H   The crow whispered, "With a magic word, you can open up the door to the Land Beneath The Mountains."

J   Rebecca steered the spacecraft slowly through the towering peaks until the landing pad came into sight.

33 One of the most difficult challenges faced by a young person learning to drive is parallel parking. This skill involves maneuvering an automobile into a parking spot so it is parallel to the curb.

Which of these is a fact that might be added to this excerpt from an informational brochure?

A   Young people are almost always nervous when they take their driver's test.

B   Bigger cars seem easier to park than smaller cars, but you really must find a space that is large enough.

C   The easiest way to parallel park is to pull ahead of the spot and back in slowly and carefully.

D   A recent study showed that more than 80% of the people surveyed prefer backing a car into a parking spot.

34 **Which of these statements makes use of a metaphor?**

F   The crowd was like a swarm of bees rushing onto the field.

G   Winning the championship was a goal that drove them all season.

H   The team held together through a season that had its ups and downs.

J   She was a gazelle, leaping over the hurdles and racing to the finish line.

STOP

Table of Contents
Language

Lesson 1   Punctuation

Examples   **Directions:** Mark the space for the punctuation mark that is
needed in the sentence. Mark the space for "None" if no more
punctuation marks are needed.

A   Jenny yelled "Watch out for the puddle!"

    A :   **B** ;   **C** ,   **D** None

B   Bread, rolls, and cereal are all good for you.

    F ?   **G** "   **H** .   **J** None

**Read the sentence, look at the answer choices, then read the
sentence again. See if any of the punctuation marks are needed in
the sentence.**

Skip difficult items and come back to them later.

Practice

1   The problem, of course is finding a job you enjoy.

    A ;   **B** .   **C** ,   **D** None

2   My family visited three states Ohio, Kentucky, and Indiana.

    F :   **G** "   **H** ,   **J** None

3   Many birds do not fly south for the winter

    A !   **B** .   **C** ?   **D** None

4   How can you be sure the bridge is safe?" asked the mayor.

    F ,   **G** "   **H** ?   **J** None

5   Yes, you will all be able to use the computer today.

    A ,   **B** !   **C** ?   **D** None

6   The hotels motels, and guest houses near the park are all expensive.

    F ,   **G** .   **H** ;   **J** None

GO ▷

For numbers 7-13, read each answer. Fill in the space for the choice that has a punctuation error. If there is no mistake, fill in the fourth answer space.

7 A   The people walking on
       B   the hiking trail did not know
       C   an owls nest was nearby.
       D   *(No mistakes)*

8 F   Harriet, the bank manager
       G   wants her workers to learn
       H   the names of their customers.
       J   *(No mistakes)*

9 A   "You are wrong," insisted
       B   Buck. "The Eagles will never
       C   win the championship."
       D   *(No mistakes)*

10 F   200 Patricia Ave
       G   Limon, UT 83123
       H   May 2, 1995
       J   *(No mistakes)*

11 A   Dear Mr. Sanford:
       B   Your company recently moved to our
       C   town! I would like to welcome you.
       D   *(No mistakes)*

12 F   As mayor, I head our development
       G   council. The members of the council
       H   are pleased you chose our town.
       J   *(No mistakes)*

13 A   We look forward to a long relationship.
       B   Sincerely
       C   *Susan Eastwick*
       D   *(No mistakes)*

For numbers 14-17, read each sentence with a blank. Choose the word or words that fit best in the blank and show the correct punctuation.

14 It's your turn to _____ Wendy.

        F   dive
        G   dive;
        H   dive,
        J   dive:

15 The rain will stop about_____ the wind
        will continue through the night.

        A   noon
        B   noon,
        C   noon:
        D   noon;

16 My _____ friend has a chance to go to
        the Olympics.

        F   sister's
        G   sisters
        H   sisters's
        J   sisters'

17 The hardware store is _____ the
        supermarket is open.

        A   closed but;
        B   closed, but
        C   closed but,
        D   closed; but

STOP

ANSWER ROWS   **7** Ⓐ Ⓑ Ⓒ Ⓓ   **10** Ⓕ Ⓖ Ⓗ Ⓙ   **13** Ⓐ Ⓑ Ⓒ Ⓓ   **16** Ⓕ Ⓖ Ⓗ Ⓙ
               8 Ⓕ Ⓖ Ⓗ Ⓙ   **11** Ⓐ Ⓑ Ⓒ Ⓓ   **14** Ⓕ Ⓖ Ⓗ Ⓙ   **17** Ⓐ Ⓑ Ⓒ Ⓓ
               9 Ⓐ Ⓑ Ⓒ Ⓓ   **12** Ⓕ Ⓖ Ⓗ Ⓙ   **15** Ⓐ Ⓑ Ⓒ Ⓓ

Examples   **Directions:** Mark the space for the answer that shows correct punctuation and capitalization. Mark the space for "Correct as it is" if the underlined part is correct.

A
A "Can we train the dog, asked Liza?

B Her mother answered, "yes but you must be firm with him."

C "Come here!" demanded Liza.

D "Now we can teach him to sit," said mother

B Tom waited for <u>Ellen and Kendall.</u>

F Ellen and, Kendall

G Ellen, and Kendall

H Ellen: and Kendall

J Correct as it is

Remember, you are looking for the answer that shows correct capitalization and punctuation.

If you are not sure which answer is correct, take your best guess.

Practice

1   A "Did you finish your project yet Asked Judy?"

B "I finished last week," answered Paco.

C My project is taking longer than I thought, added Judy."

D "I would be happy to help", suggested Paco.

2   F The bank on the corner isn't open yet.

G On which Street is the supermarket?

H The parking lot you are looking for is just a few blocks away

J We'll meet for lunch at the Restaurant beside the park.

3   A Many Americans' visit Canada and Mexico, our nearest neighbors.

B Its sometimes cheaper to fly from new York to London than to Arizona.

C You might be surprised to learn that Africa has snow-capped mountains.

D people in China are learning more about democracy and free enterprise.

4   The <u>river however</u> is too high for safe boating.

F river, however,

G river, however

H river however,

J Correct as it is

5   Nadine lives in an apartment <u>building with</u> a garden on the roof.

A building, with

B building: with

C building; with

D Correct as it is

6   The <u>bears</u> cubs followed behind her.

F bears's

G bears'

H bear's

J Correct as it is

GO ▶

(7)   Did you ever wonder how public transportation began? A

(8)   business owner in france, set up a stage line between the center of

(9)   the Town of Nantes; and a public bathing house he owned. He

discovered that people were more interested in riding his

(10)   "omnibus" than in bathing. He started a new business. That was

quickly imitated in other cities.

7   A   began. A
    B   began, a
    C   began: a
    D   Correct as it is

9   A   town of Nantes,
    B   town, of Nantes,
    C   town of Nantes
    D   Correct as it is

8   F   France set
    G   France, set
    H   France. Set
    J   Correct as it is

10   F   business, that
     G   business that
     H   business that,
     J   Correct as it is

---

(11)   March, 4, 1995

      National Stove Co.

(12)   899 Harvest St

      Olson, Montana 59064

      Dear Mr. Tingley:

(13)   Our school has a stove made by your company in 1884, we

      would like to know if you have a catalog from that time. My class

      thinks it would be great to learn the history of our stove.

(14)   sincerely yours

                                              Jane Gibbons

11   A   march 4 1995,
     B   March 4 1995,
     C   March 4, 1995
     D   Correct as it is

13   A   1884: we
     B   1884. We
     C   1884 we
     D   Correct as it is

12   F   899 Harvest St:
     G   899 Harvest St.
     H   899 Harvest St,
     J   Correct as it is

14   F   Sincerely yours,
     G   Sincerely Yours:
     H   Sincerely Yours
     J   Correct as it is

GO

For numbers 15 and 16, read the sentence with a blank. Mark the space beside the answer choice that fits best in the blank and has correct capitalization and punctuation.

15 The highway near our _____ rarely has much traffic.

 A house, Route 165,
 B house; Route 165
 C house. route 165,
 D house, route 165

16 The mountain we planned to climb is located _____ .

 F west of cheyenne
 G West of Cheyenne
 H west of Cheyenne
 J West of cheyenne

Victor wrote this report about space travel. Read the report and use it to do numbers 17-20.

> People have dreamed about traveling in space for
> **(1)**
> hundred's of years. It is only recently however
> **(2)**
> that space travel became a reality. The first space
> **(3)**
> traveler was Yuri Gagarin. In 1961, this cosmonaut
> **(4)**
> from the former soviet union orbited the earth in a
> satellite. Since Gagarin's flight, hundreds of
> **(5)**
> others have flown in space, and more than a dozen
> people have gone as far as the moon.

17 In sentence 1, hundred's of years is best written —

 A hundred's of year's
 B hundreds of years
 C hundreds of years'
 D As it is

18 In sentence 2, recently however is best written —

 F recently, however,
 G recently however,
 H recently. However
 J As it is

19 In sentence 4, soviet union orbited is best written —

 A Soviet union orbited
 B Soviet Union. Orbited
 C Soviet Union orbited
 D As it is

20 In sentence 5, Gagarin's flight, is best written —

 F Gagarins flight
 G Gagarins flight;
 H Gagarins' flight;
 J As it is

ANSWER ROWS **15** Ⓐ Ⓑ Ⓒ Ⓓ   **17** Ⓐ Ⓑ Ⓒ Ⓓ   **19** Ⓐ Ⓑ Ⓒ Ⓓ
             16 Ⓕ Ⓖ Ⓗ Ⓙ   **18** Ⓕ Ⓖ Ⓗ Ⓙ   **20** Ⓕ Ⓖ Ⓗ Ⓙ

Example   **Directions:** Fill in the answer circle for the punctuation mark that is needed in the sentence. If no punctuation mark is needed fill in the answer circle for the word "None".

E1

    Yes there is fruit in the refrigerator.

    A ,   **B** ;   **C** :   **D** None

1   The contractor fixed several things the leaky roof, the loose tiles, and the broken window.

    A ,   **B** ;   **C** :   **D** None

2   "How have you been" asked Uncle Akim.

    F ?   **G** ,   **H** !   **J** None

3   The front seat is so full of boxes that I can't shut the car door.

    A :   **B** ,   **C** ;   **D** None

4   The price which was printed on the box, included all state and local taxes.

    F ;   **G** ,   **H** :   **J** None

For numbers 5-7, read each answer. Fill in the space for the choice that has a punctuation error. If there is no mistake, fill in the fourth answer space.

5 **A**   The sidewalk, which
    B was covered with wet
    C leaves was very slippery.
    D *(No mistakes)*

6 **F**   This basketball is mine.
    G Viviens is in the closet or
    H on the shelf in the basement.
    J *(No mistakes)*

7 **A**   No matter what we try,"
    B complained Stu, "the flowers
    C we planted don't do well."
    D *(No mistakes)*

For numbers 8 and 9, read each sentence with a blank. Choose the word or words that fit best in the blank and show the correct punctuation.

8   Most runners enjoy their_____ feel bad if they miss a day.

    F sport. they
    G sport, they
    H sport: they
    J sport; they

9   Ocean _____ large amounts of sand from one place to another.

    A current's move
    B currents' move
    C currents move
    D currents, move

GO ▷

ANSWER ROWS **E1** Ⓐ Ⓑ Ⓒ Ⓓ   **2** Ⓕ Ⓖ Ⓗ Ⓙ   **4** Ⓕ Ⓖ Ⓗ Ⓙ   **6** Ⓕ Ⓖ Ⓗ Ⓙ   **8** Ⓕ Ⓖ Ⓗ Ⓙ
           1 Ⓐ Ⓑ Ⓒ Ⓓ   **3** Ⓐ Ⓑ Ⓒ Ⓓ   **5** Ⓐ Ⓑ Ⓒ Ⓓ   **7** Ⓐ Ⓑ Ⓒ Ⓓ   **9** Ⓐ Ⓑ Ⓒ Ⓓ

63

For numbers 10-13, read each group of sentences. Find the one that is written correctly and shows the correct capitalization and punctuation.

10 F Corine called, and wants to know if you saw *desert rescue*.

   G The movie was good, but the ticket price was too high.

   H My friends and I, go to the Movies about once a week.

   J We pay for our movie tickets, by working on saturday.

11 A You shouldnt' worry about finishing your painting today.

   B Nancys drawing has a lot of detail.

   C Many people have more artistic talent, than they think.

   D Your painting is beautiful, Willie.

12 F Vachel wondered, "where does the water in this lake come from?"

   G "It always seems to be full said Alberto.

   H "That small stream," Earlene commented, "dries up in the summer."

   J "I think it is fed by a spring," suggested Hunter

13 A A desk, chair, and bookcase will cost about a thousand dollars.

   B The furniture you ordered, will arrive next week.

   C Which will cost the most a bed dresser or chair?

   D When the furniture is delivered, my sister, and I will help move it.

For numbers 14-17, read the sentence with a blank. Mark the space beside the answer choice that fits best in the blank and has correct capitalization and punctuation.

14 Here is what the estimate will _____ labor, materials, and taxes.

   F include:
   G include,
   H include;
   J include

15 Randolph _____ begins on the west side of the city and continues to the river.

   A AVE
   B Ave.
   C AVE.
   D ave.

16 Most of us brought _____ forgot his and got soaked.

   F umbrellas but George
   G umbrellas, but George
   H umbrellas. But George
   J umbrellas, But George

17 A _____ will be built on the site of the old brick factory.

   A City Park
   B City park
   C city Park
   D city park

GO

For numbers 18-21, look at the underlined part of each sentence. Find the answer choice that shows the correct capitalization and punctuation for the underlined part.

18 Which of the <u>teams'</u> do you think will win the championship?

   F team's

   G teams's

   H teams

   J Correct as it is

19 "The gas tank on the lawn mower is almost <u>empty" Warned</u> Donna.

   A empty." Warned

   B empty," warned

   C empty warned,"

   D Correct as it is

20 The lamp is <u>broken, but</u> I think it can be fixed.

   F broken. But

   G broken but,

   H broken but

   J Correct as it is

21 The company's <u>workers managers,</u> and owners all helped it succeed.

   A workers, managers,

   B workers, Managers

   C Workers, Managers

   D Correct as it is

For numbers 22-25, read the passage. Find the answer choice that shows the correct capitalization and punctuation for the underlined part.

(22)   Is it possible for humans to fly under their own <u>power. The</u>

(23)   answer is <u>yes but</u> not for all humans and not for very far. Under good conditions, a well-conditioned athlete can pedal a specially designed plane and remain aloft for up to thirty miles. A series of

(24)   gears transfers the <u>person's energy</u> from the pedals to a propeller. This pushes the pedal-plane forward fast enough for the person to

(25)   remain aloft for <u>short, periods, of time</u>.

22 **F** power? The
   G power; the
   H power, the
   J Correct as it is

23 **A** yes; But
   B yes: but
   C yes, but
   D Correct as it is

24 **F** persons energy
   G persons' energy
   H Person's energy
   J Correct as it is

25 **A** short periods, of time
   B short periods of time
   C short, periods of time
   D Correct as it is

GO

ANSWER ROWS   **18** Ⓕ Ⓖ Ⓗ Ⓙ   **20** Ⓕ Ⓖ Ⓗ Ⓙ   **22** Ⓕ Ⓖ Ⓗ Ⓙ   **24** Ⓕ Ⓖ Ⓗ Ⓙ
             19 Ⓐ Ⓑ Ⓒ Ⓓ   **21** Ⓐ Ⓑ Ⓒ Ⓓ   **23** Ⓐ Ⓑ Ⓒ Ⓓ   **25** Ⓐ Ⓑ Ⓒ Ⓓ

65

This is more of Victor's report about space travel. Read the report and use it to do numbers 26-29.

Spacecraft today are powered by rockets that
(1)
burn lots of fuel and take off from earth. Many
(2)
scientists believe that this method is'nt very

sensible. They suggest that we build space stations
(3)
hundreds of miles from earth. These space stations
(4)
would serve as research labs assembly plants, and

launch sites.

The logic behind a space station is simple.
(5)
Although it requires a great deal of power to
(6)
launch a rocket from the earth, very little power

is needed to launch a rocket from an orbiting space

station. This means that much larger spacecraft
(7)
could be constructed and launched for the long

voyage to mars or other planets.

26 In sentence 2, method is'nt is best written —

F   method. Is'nt
G   method isn't
H   method isnt'
J   As it is

27 In sentence 4, labs assembly is best written —

A   labs, assembly
B   labs assembly;
C   labs assembly,
D   As it is

28 In sentence 6, earth, very is best written —

F   earth. Very
G   earth very,
H   earth: very
J   As it is

29 In sentence 7, mars or other planets is best written —

A   Mars or other Planets
B   mars or other Planets
C   Mars or other planets
D   As it is

STOP

Lesson 4   Usage

Examples   **Directions:** Read the directions for each section. Fill in the circle for the answer you think is correct.

Choose the word or phrase that best completes the sentence.	Choose the answer that is a complete and correctly written sentence.

A Our class _____ a trip to the beach since we started school in September.
 	
  A will be planning
  B plans
  C has been planning
  D were planning
	B **F** The tastiest tomatoes are grown at home.
	     G Which of the five plants grew faster?
	     H We'll have to dig a deepest hole to plant this tree.
	     J Some people in the city plant a smaller garden in a window box.

Tips

If you are not sure which answer choice is correct, say each one to yourself. The right answer usually sounds best.

If you are still not sure which answer choice is correct, eliminate answers you know are wrong and then take your best guess.

Practice

For numbers 1-3, choose the word or phrase that best completes the sentence.

1 The horse walked from _____ .

  A she to me

  B her to me

  C she to I

  D her to I

2 The rain, _____ we needed, finally came.

  F which

  G who

  H when

  J what

3 The street lights _____ soon.

  A did come on

  B come on

  C came on

  D will come on

For numbers 4-6, choose the answer that is a complete and correctly written sentence.

4 **F** The door works because Lenore fixed them yesterday.

    G My brother baked cookies and brought it to school yesterday.

    H The crossing guard wears a hat to protect her from the sun.

    J My friend lost its backpack on a hike in the mountains.

5 **A** Bev brang her cousin to the game.

    B Let's set here under the tree.

    C Are they goin to finish soon?

    D The wind blew the chairs over.

6 **F** The children played happier on the lawn.

    G The moon is shining brightly tonight.

    H I scraped my arm on a roughest stone.

    J Is that knife sharply enough?

GO

For numbers 7-12, read each answer choice. Fill in the space for the choice that has a usage error. If there is no mistake, fill in the fourth answer space.

7   **A**   Although she looked in many stores,
    B   Marilyn couldn't find her a pair of
    C   running shoes that felt comfortable.
    D   *(No mistakes)*

8   **F**   Roddy must of noticed
    G   the flat tire, so he took the
    H   bus to work instead of driving.
    J   *(No mistakes)*

9   **A**   The supermarket on the corner
    B   weren't open when we stopped
    C   there last night about ten o'clock.
    D   *(No mistakes)*

10   **F**   The simplest way to become
    G   good at a sport is to learn about
    H   it and to practice often.
    J   *(No mistakes)*

11   **A**   The airplane has been parked
    B   on the runway for an hour waiting
    C   for a gate has become available.
    D   *(No mistakes)*

12   **F**   Your more likely to
    G   cut yourself using a dull
    H   knife than a sharp one.
    J   *(No mistakes)*

For numbers 13 and 14, choose the best way to write the underlined part of each sentence. If the underlined part is correct, fill in the fourth answer space.

13   We can take a walk **however** the turkey is cooking in the oven.

    A   during
    B   after
    C   while
    D   *(No change)*

14   A good way to make friends is to **express an interest** in what people do.

    F   express and interest
    G   express interested
    H   express interesting
    J   *(No change)*

For numbers 15 and 16, choose the answer that is a complete and correctly written sentence.

15   **A**   The plants are doing well, even though the soil doesn't seem very rich.
    B   Although it is late, light enough to take the dog for a walk.
    C   As we pulled away from the house, and Joan arrived then.
    D   How do you know which of these is best unless trying it first?

16   **F**   Over a hundred feet tall, the worker climbed to the top of the tower.
    G   The dentist's office called, for to see how you were doing.
    H   Flapping its wings, the farmer tried to catch the chicken.
    J   Janelle runs every day, even if the weather is terrible.

GO >

Here is more of the report Victor wrote about space travel. Read the report and use it to do numbers 17-20.

An interesting aspect of space travel is the
(1)
great distances involved. The distance to our
(2)
neighboring planets is measuring in millions of

miles, and to the stars in a unit called a "light-

year." Scientists define a light-year as the
(3)
distance a beam of light can travel in one year;

it is approximately six trillion miles.

   Because of the huge distances involved, it is
(4)
unlike that people will travel to the stars anytime

in the near future. It is possible, however, that
(5)
humans will land on another planet in our lifetime.

Currently, plans are being considered to land a
(6)
crew on the planet Mars. Even traveling at 20,000
(7)
miles an hour, it has taken months to travel from

the earth to Mars.

17 In sentence 2, <u>is measuring</u> is best written —

  A is measured
  B measured
  C was measuring
  D As it is

18 In sentence 3, <u>it is</u> is best written —

  F it will be
  G they are
  H they will be
  J As it is

19 In sentence 4, <u>unlike</u> is best written —

  A dislikes
  B unlikely
  C unliked
  D As it is

20 In sentence 7, <u>has taken</u> is best written —

  F was taking
  G have taken
  H will take
  J As it is

STOP

Examples   **Directions:** Read the directions for each section. Fill in the circle for the answer you think is correct.

Which word is the simple subject of the sentence?
 	
A   A fallen tree blocked the highway.
        A **B** **C**   **D**
 	
Which word is the simple predicate (verb) of the sentence?
 	
B   The otter slowly paddled toward shore.
        F   **G**   **H**   **J**
	Which answer choice is the best combination of the underlined sentences?
	
	C The table is new.
	        The table is in the dining room.
	
	  A The new table that is in the dining room.
	  B The table is in the new dining room.
	  C The table in the dining room is new.
	  D In the dining room is the new table.

If a question is too difficult, skip it and come back to it later.

Stay with your first answer choice. You should change an answer only if you are sure the new one is correct.

Practice

For numbers 1-3, find the underlined part that is the simple subject of the sentence.

1   Clouds often form in the afternoon in many places around the world.
      A   **B**   **C**   **D**

2   Twelve beautiful trees lined the street.
      F   **G**   **H**   **J**

3   With her basketball in her hand, Christie jogged toward the court.
           A   **B**   **C**   **D**

For numbers 4-6, find the underlined part that is the simple predicate (verb) of the sentence.

4   The rod slipped from Mark's hand into the water.
        F **G**   **H**   **J**

5   Talented sports stars earn very large salaries.
      A   **B**   **C**   **D**

6   A nicely framed picture hung on the wall above the desk.
      F   **G**   **H**   **J**

GO

For numbers 7-9, choose the answer that best combines the underlined sentences.

7   A bird visited our feeder.

   The bird had a crest and a long tail.

   A   A bird with a crest and a long tail visited our feeder.

   B   A bird visited our feeder that had a crest and a long tail.

   C   Having a crest and a long tail, a bird visited our feeder.

   D   The bird that visited our feeder, it had a crest and a long tail.

8   Lisa sometimes helps her father fix their car.

   Lisa is in my science class.

   F   Lisa sometimes helps her father fix their car, who is in my science class.

   G   Sometimes helping her father fix their car, Lisa is in my science class.

   H   In my science class, Lisa sometimes helps her father fix their car.

   J   Lisa, who is in my science class, sometimes helps her father fix their car.

9   The small stream is near our house.

   The stream is usually about a foot deep.

   The stream sometimes floods the neighborhood.

   A   The small stream is near our house and is usually about a foot deep and sometimes floods the neighborhood.

   B   The small stream near our house, which is usually about a foot deep, sometimes floods the neighborhood.

   C   Our neighborhood is sometimes flooded, but the stream is usually only about a foot deep.

   D   The stream that sometimes floods the nearby neighborhood is usually about a foot deep.

For numbers 10 and 11, choose the best way of expressing the idea.

10   **F**   Many people who are more athletic than when they were working are retired.
   G   Many retired people who are more athletic except when they were working.
   H   Many retired people are more athletic than when they were working.
   J   Many people, when they retire, although they are more athletic than working.

11   **A**   Remember that when you call home, you should arrive at soccer camp.
   B   Remember to call home as soon as you arrive at soccer camp.
   C   Remember to arrive at soccer camp and call home soon.
   D   As soon as you remember to arrive at soccer camp, you should call home.

GO

ANSWER ROW   7 Ⓐ Ⓑ Ⓒ Ⓓ   8 Ⓕ Ⓖ Ⓗ Ⓙ   9 Ⓐ Ⓑ Ⓒ Ⓓ   10 Ⓕ Ⓖ Ⓗ Ⓙ   11 Ⓐ Ⓑ Ⓒ Ⓓ   71

Victor's report about space travel continues here. Use it to do numbers 12-15.

```
              Taking a long space flight, it is not at all
          (1)
      like it is taking a long plane ride. These two
                                               (2)
      things are very different, as you will see. For one
                                                    (3)
      thing, a plane ride is rarely more than twelve

      hours long. A space flight would last for months or
                (4)
      even years. In a plane, if an emergency occurs, you
                  (5)
      can usually find a place to land. There is no such
                                         (6)
      thing as an emergency landing in a space craft. You
                                                       (7)
      will be too far from earth. You will also be too
                  (8)
      far from any other planet that can support life. A
                                                      (9)
      plane lands every few hours, where it is resupplied

      with food, water, and fuel. A space ship would have
                                    (10)
      to carry all the fuel, food, and water the

      travelers need.
```

12 How is sentence 1 best written?

F Like a long plane ride, taking a long space flight is not alike.

G It is not alike, like taking a long space flight and a long plane ride.

H Taking a long space flight is not at all like taking a long plane ride.

J As it is

13 How can sentences 7 and 8 best be combined without changing their meaning?

A You will be too far from earth or any other planet that can support life.

B Too far from earth, you will also be too far from any other planet that can support life.

C The earth is far from any other planet that can support life.

D You will be too far from earth, a planet that can support life.

14 How is sentence 9 best written?

F A plane lands every few hours. Where it is resupplied with food, water, and fuel.

G A plane, where it is resupplied with food, water, and fuel, can land every few hours.

H Resupplying a plane with food, water, and fuel, it lands every few hours.

J As it is

15 Which sentence needlessly repeats an idea?

A 2

B 3

C 5

D 6

72

STOP

Example   **Directions:** Read the directions for each section. Fill in the circle for the answer you think is correct.

Read the paragraph below. Find the best topic sentence for the paragraph.

A   _____ . William Seward, the Secretary of State for President Andrew Johnson, negotiated a treaty to acquire Alaska for $7.2 million in gold. At the time, many people thought the price was too high and called the purchase "Seward's Folly." Today, Alaska generates more than $7.2 million dollars each day in natural resources.

    A Alaska deserves its reputation as "The Last Frontier."

    B It took almost a century from the time Alaska was purchased until it became a state.

    C Few people ever associate Alaska with President Andrew Johnson.

    D The purchase of Alaska from Russia was an incredible bargain.

Remember, a paragraph should focus on one idea. The correct answer is the one that fits best with the rest of the paragraph.

If you are not sure which answer is correct, try each answer choice in the blank. Choose the one that sounds the best.

Practice

Read the paragraph below. Find the best topic sentence for the paragraph.

1   _____ . When she was young, she saw him almost every week because he lived nearby. For the past six years, however, Uncle Nicholas had been stationed overseas in the Air Force.

    A Maria didn't know what to expect.

    B It had been years since Maria had seen her uncle.

    C Maria's Uncle Nicholas was considered by everyone to be a strange character.

    D Every family has someone who is considered a character.

Find the answer choice that best develops the topic sentence below.

2   The Dust Bowl is the name given to a section of the American West in the 1930s.

    F The area's problems were worsened because of the Great Depression. Many people lost their savings in the stock market crash.

    G Much of the problem was the result of poor agricultural practices. We have learned better farming techniques today, so it probably won't happen again.

    H The region included parts of Oklahoma, Texas, Colorado, Kansas, and New Mexico. Many people migrated from the region to California.

    J The region, which included a number of states, was devastated by drought from 1934 to 1937. High winds blew millions of tons of soil into the air, creating huge dust storms.

GO

For numbers 3 and 4, read the paragraph. Find the sentence that does not belong in the paragraph.

3   1. The floor plan of a home determines how livable it is.   2. The kitchen, for example, should be close to the dining room.   3. Bedrooms are best located far from the kitchen or living room so they will be quiet.   4. Most families find that they use one room more than any other.

A Sentence 1

B Sentence 2

C Sentence 3

D Sentence 4

4   1. Natalie was very disappointed at what had happened to her.   2. She lived in a small town with her parents and two brothers.   3. During a basketball game, she had hurt her knee.   4. Not only would it require surgery, but it also meant she would be unable to join her class on a trip to Virginia Beach.

F Sentence 1

G Sentence 2

H Sentence 3

J Sentence 4

For numbers 5 and 6, read the paragraph. Find the sentence that best fits the blank in the paragraph.

5   A remarkable event occurred on Halloween evening in 1938. At that time, there was no television, and most Americans depended on radio for their information and entertainment. _____ . The show was so convincing that millions of people thought the earth had been invaded by Martians.

A Families often gathered around the radio to enjoy an evening together.

B Orson Welles, producer of *War of the Worlds*, also made famous movies.

C *War of the Worlds*, a radio program, later was made into a successful movie.

D A program named *War of the Worlds* was broadcast on the radio.

6   In the early 1950s, a tiny champion nicknamed "Little Mo" changed women's tennis forever. Maureen Connolly was a powerful player who hit harder than any woman had before. _____. From 1952 through 1954, she was named woman athlete of the year by sportswriters.

F She won four major championships in one year, the "grand slam" of tennis.

G Connolly began playing tennis at the age of ten.

H Her career ended when she injured her leg in a horseback riding accident.

J She won the first tennis tournament she ever entered.

For numbers 7-9, use the paragraph below to answer the questions.

> ¹If you take a closer look, however, you will be surprised at what you find. ²In the distance, a huge polar bear is wandering in great circles sniffing the wind. ³On the ground, a snowy owl is watching carefully over its three chicks. ⁴The bear is searching for its favorite prey, a seal. ⁵Some of the residents of the far north live there all year, but others migrate south for the long winter.

7   Choose the best opening sentence to add to this paragraph.

   A The coldest places on earth are the north and south polar regions.
   B At first glance, the snow-covered Arctic seems lifeless.
   C Animals have adapted to some of the harshest places on earth.
   D Even in the summer, the Arctic is covered with a blanket of snow.

8   Which sentence should be left out of this paragraph?

   F Sentence 1
   G Sentence 4
   H Sentence 3
   J Sentence 5

9   Where is the best place for sentence 4?

   A Where it is now
   B Between sentences 1 and 2
   C Between sentences 2 and 3
   D After sentence 5

10 Which of the following would be most appropriate at the beginning of a report on the Louisiana Purchase?

   F On October 20, 1803, the United States Senate approved the purchase of more than 800,000 square miles of land from France. The Louisiana Purchase, as it came to be known, more than doubled the size of the young nation and opened up the possibility of a huge western expansion.

   G Within a year of completing the Louisiana Purchase, President Thomas Jefferson commissioned Meriwether Lewis and William Clark to explore the new region. Their trip became one of the most celebrated adventures in American history.

   H Most people think of the southern states as being the bulk of the Louisiana Purchase. These states were certainly part of the Louisiana Territory, but so were regions of the far north, including the Dakotas and parts of Montana and Wyoming.

   J The Louisiana Purchase was important for several reasons. Most obviously, it added huge territory to the United States, more than 800,000 square miles. It also gave the young nation a port on the Gulf of Mexico and split the territory that was claimed by Spain.

GO

Here is more of Victor's report about space travel. Use the story to do numbers 11-14.

Space travel has many unusual aspects. One of
(1)   (2)
the most challenging is dealing with a condition

called "weightlessness." Also known as "zero-G" or
(3)
zero gravity, weightlessness is the result of being

so far from a planet or star that there is almost

no gravity. This sounds like fun because you can
(4)
fly, but it has great disadvantages. Liquids don't
(5)
pour, and in fact break into tiny droplets that get

all over everything. The human body doesn't respond
(6)
very well to weightlessness. Exercise is important
(7)
to good muscle tone. Without gravity, a body
(8)
doesn't have to work very hard and muscles soon

lose their tone. Even veins and arteries become
(9)
weaker so that the risk of circulatory problems

increases.

11 **Which sentence could be added before sentence 4?**

A Gravity is still a mystery that scientists don't understand well.
B The bigger the planet, the greater the force of gravity.
C People and objects simply float in space.
D You can't actually see gravity.

12 **What is the topic sentence of this paragraph?**

F 1
G 2
H 3
J 4

13 **What supporting information could be added after sentence 5?**

A Because of this, you can only drink liquids from a squeeze bottle.
B The three most common forms of matter are gas, liquid, and solid.
C Solids are not affected as much.
D Water would still freeze at 32° F.

14 **Which sentence contains information that does *not* belong in the story?**

F 2
G 3
H 6
J 7

76

STOP

Example   Directions: Find the underlined part that is the simple subject of the sentence.

E1

Two patients waited in the dentist's office.
  A   B   C   D

For number 1, choose the word or phrase that best completes the sentence.

1   The taxi _____ and is waiting for you outside the lobby door.

    A is arriving

    B will arrive

    C arrives

    D has arrived

For number 2, choose the answer that is a complete and correctly written sentence.

2   **F** The manager didn't want nobody to bring food into the store.

    G We gotta wait a few minutes until Doug makes a phone call.

    H The book about flying that you are interested in is now in stock.

    J If you will leave us go to the mall, we will be back by four o'clock.

For numbers 3-5, read each answer choice. Fill in the space for the choice that has a usage error. If there is no mistake, fill in the fourth answer space.

3   **A**   Samantha rung the bell several
    B times, but nobody answered.
    C I guess they weren't home.
    D *(No mistakes)*

4   **F**   It's hard to believe, but Arlo
    G hurt hiself getting out of
    H bed yesterday morning.
    J *(No mistakes)*

5   **A**   As flimsy as a spider's web
    B looks, it is surprisingly
    C strong and durable.
    D *(No mistakes)*

For number 6, find the underlined part that is the simple subject of the sentence.

6   A few weeks ago the mayor announced the construction of a new town hall.
     F   G   H   J

For number 7, find the underlined part that is the simple predicate (verb) of the sentence.

7   Buffalo roamed throughout much of the West until the late nineteenth century.
     A   B   C   D

GO ▷

ANSWER ROWS   **E1** (A) (B) (C) (D)   **2** (F) (G) (H) (J)   **4** (F) (G) (H) (J)   **6** (F) (G) (H) (J)
                   1 (A) (B) (C) (D)   **3** (A) (B) (C) (D)   **5** (A) (B) (C) (D)   **7** (A) (B) (C) (D)

77

For numbers 8-10, choose the answer that best combines the underlined sentences.

8   The carpenter used redwood to build a deck.

Redwood looks nice and doesn't rot.

    F The carpenter, who built the deck, because redwood looks nice and doesn't rot.

    G Because it looks nice and doesn't rot, the deck was built by the carpenter of redwood.

    H Redwood looks nice and doesn't rot, but the carpenter used it to build a deck.

    J The carpenter used redwood to build a deck because it looks nice and doesn't rot.

9   The dog is not allowed on the furniture.

We think she gets up on the furniture when we are not home.

    A The dog is not allowed on the furniture, on which we think she gets when we are not home.

    B The dog is not allowed on the furniture, but we think she gets up on it when we are not home.

    C We think the dog gets up on the furniture when we are not home, and she is not allowed to.

    D Although she is not allowed on the furniture, but we think she does when we are not home.

10   My mother is opening a business.

She will sell coffee and sandwiches.

The business will be in the new shopping center.

    F My mother is opening a business selling coffee and sandwiches in the new shopping center.

    G My mother, who is opening a business, selling coffee and sandwiches in the new shopping center.

    H The business in the new shopping center will be my mother's who will sell coffee and sandwiches.

    J Selling coffee and sandwiches, my mother is opening a business in the new shopping center.

For numbers 11 and 12, choose the best way of expressing the idea.

11 **A** For to wash the windows, you will have to borrow a ladder.
    B If you are going to wash the windows, you will have to borrow a ladder.
    C You will have to borrow a ladder. Although you are going to wash the windows.
    D After you borrow a ladder, you will have to wash the windows.

12 **F** The plane took off late, although there was a storm at its destination.
    G The plane took off late because of a storm at its destination.
    H The plane, which took off late, and a storm was at its destination.
    J The plane that took off late, which had a storm at its destination.

GO

Read the paragraph below. Find the best topic sentence for the paragraph.

13 _____ . The inside of the plant is like a sponge that holds water during long dry spells. The outside of the cactus is a waxy skin that prevents water inside the plant from evaporating during hot days. The sharp spines of a cactus prevent animals from eating them.

   A For a short period of time in the spring, a cactus plant has a beautiful flower.

   B Some cactus plants in the Arizona desert are hundreds of years old.

   C Cactus plants are perfectly adapted to a desert environment.

   D Experienced desert travelers know that a cactus plant is an important source of water.

Find the answer choice that best develops the topic sentence.

14 Lani had lots to do in order to get ready for her party.

   F She and her mother had to buy the food and prepare it. Lani also had to find time to clean the house, as she had promised her mother she would.

   G She had invited more than twenty of her friends. The party was to welcome the exchange student who would live with Lani's family.

   H The party would take place on Friday evening. The exchange student, Guillermo, would arrive Friday morning.

   J There would be more than twenty of her friends at the party. Some of them had invited Lani to parties at their houses.

Read the paragraph below. Find the sentence that does not belong in the paragraph.

15 1. Each year, the families in Ira's neighborhood have a picnic.   2. The purpose of the picnic is for the families to get to know one another better.   3. Other neighborhoods use different activities to achieve the same purpose.   4. The picnic begins about noon and includes sports, games, and lots of food.

   A Sentence 1

   B Sentence 2

   C Sentence 3

   D Sentence 4

Read the paragraph below. Find the sentence that best fits the blank in the paragraph.

16   In New York, there is a museum dedicated to American folk art. _____ . Folk art is usually simpler than traditional art, and often includes practical objects. Many of the people who are folk artists are self-trained and pursue their art for their own pleasure.

   F Other countries have their own forms of folk art.

   G New York is also the home to many other famous or unusual museums.

   H A magazine about folk art named the *Clarion* is published by the museum.

   J This form of art includes things such as carvings, paintings, calligraphy, and quilts.

GO ▷

Below is the conclusion of Victor's report about space travel. Read the conclusion and use it to do numbers 17-20.

Within the next ten years, it is almost certain
(1)
that a manned spaceflight <u>will reach</u> the planet

Mars. The mission, which will probably be made up
(2)
of crew members, who are from several nations. They
(3)
will spend a short period of time on the Red

Planet, set up an automated research station, and

return to earth.

At the same time preparations are being made for
(4)
the Mars flight, a space station will be under

construction. Again, the problem of zero gravity
(5)
will have to be overcome. It is from this space
(6)
station that the serious exploration of our solar

system will be made. The next step, of course, will
(7)
be travel to another star, a step that is at least

a hundred years away.

---

17 In sentence 1, <u>will reach</u> is best written —

A reaching
B had reached
C reaches
D As it is

18 How is sentence 2 best written?

F The mission will probably be made up of crew members from several nations.
G From several nations, crew members will probably be made up.
H The mission's crew, which will be made up of members from several nations.
J As it is

19 Which sentence could be added after sentence 3?

A Mars is too harsh to support human life.
B The Mars explorers will surely be glad to return to earth.
C A huge crowd will welcome them home.
D Their trip will be mostly symbolic, but will mark humankind's first interplanetary adventure.

20 Which of these sentences does not belong in this report?

F 1
G 5
H 6
J 7

80

Examples **Directions:** Follow the directions for each section. Choose the answer you think is correct.

Find the word that is spelled correctly and fits best in the sentence.	Choose the phrase in which the underlined word is <u>not</u> spelled correctly.
A The sun is a source of cheap _____ .	**B** **F** <u>gradual</u> change
A inergy	**G** find it <u>troublesome</u>
B energy	**H** <u>speciel</u> friend
C enirgy	**J** traffic <u>barrier</u>
D energie	

Read the directions carefully. Be sure you know if you should look for the correctly spelled word or the incorrectly spelled word.

If you are not sure which answer is correct, look at each choice and say it to yourself. Choose the one that looks or sounds best.

Practice

For numbers 1-5, find the word that is spelled correctly and fits best in the blank.

1 The _____ of this car is high.

A qualaty
B quallity
C qualety
D quality

2 I have never visited a _____ country.

F foreign
G forein
H forin
J foriegn

3 Can you _____ your teacher?

A imitate
B imatate
C emitate
D imitait

4 This store has been _____ for a year.

F vacent
G vackant
H vacant
J vaicant

5 Did I _____ we will have a party?

A mansion
B mention
C mension
D menshun

For numbers 6-8, read the phrases. Choose the phrase in which the underlined word is not spelled correctly.

6 **F** <u>worthless</u> junk

G smooth <u>serface</u>

H quickly <u>accelerate</u>

J <u>musical</u> instrument

7 **A** useful <u>conference</u>

B <u>predictable</u> end

C long <u>delay</u>

D <u>encredible</u> sight

8 **F** <u>notise</u> something

G <u>rarely</u> visit

H <u>important</u> discovery

J easy <u>solution</u>

GO ⟩

For numbers 9-11, read each answer. Fill in the space for the choice that has a spelling error. If there is no mistake, fill in the last answer space.

9 **A** coastline
   B equipment
   C occupation
   D hesitate
   E *(No mistakes)*

10 **F** original
   G wholsome
   H popular
   J weaken
   K *(No mistakes)*

11 **A** natural
   B access
   C curious
   D responsability
   E *(No mistakes)*

For numbers 12-14, read each phrase. One of the underlined words is not spelled correctly for the way it is used in the phrase. Fill in the space for the word that is not spelled correctly.

12 **F** work all weak
   G always polite
   H can't locate
   J arrest a criminal

13 **A** accomplish a goal
   B seem bright
   C soar knee
   D famous picture

14 **F** good conduct
   G raise of the sun
   H certain victory
   J clear evidence

For numbers 15-18, find the underlined part that is misspelled. If all of the words are spelled correctly, mark the space under No mistake.

15 We were <u>completly</u> taken by <u>surprise</u> by the <u>sudden</u> storm. <u>No mistake.</u>
        A   B   C   D

16 Harry couldn't <u>understand</u> the <u>diegram</u> explaining how to <u>assemble</u> the bicycle. <u>No mistake.</u>
                       F   G   H   J

17 A <u>local</u> <u>merchant</u> offered a discount to students who <u>achieved</u> good grades. <u>No mistake.</u>
          A   B   C   D

18 The <u>police</u> <u>doubted</u> the story told by the <u>suspect</u>. <u>No mistake.</u>
            F   G   H   J

STOP

Lesson 9   Test Yourself

Example   **Directions:** For E1, fill in the space for the word that is spelled correctly and fits best in the sentence. For E2, choose the phrase in which the underlined word is misspelled.

E1

Be _____ on the way home.

A caustious
B caucious
C cautus
D cautious

E2

F hazerdous road
G become crowded
H late departure
J gather together

For numbers 1-6, find the word that is spelled correctly and fits best in the blank.

1 The _____ will be held next month.

A alection
B election
C eletion
D elecktion

2 What is that _____ sound?

F annoing
G annoyeing
H annoying
J anoying

3 The _____ lasted many weeks.

A jerney
B jurney
C hournie
D journey

4 The _____ pleased everyone.

F agrement
G agreemint
H agreement
J aggreement

5 This computer has an _____ disk drive.

A internal
B internel
C enternal
D entirnal

6 Allen taught his dog to _____ well.

F behaiv
G behaive
H behav
J behave

For numbers 7-10, read the phrases. Choose the phrase in which the underlined word is not spelled correctly.

7 A become famous
   B feel accitement
   C stay inactive
   D modern conveniences

8 F nutritious lunch
   G warning sign
   H free tickit
   J remain fearless

9 A relaible automobile
   B much enjoyment
   C incorrect form
   D difficult obstacle

10 F sense of pride
   G reason for leaving
   H great advantige
   J confused about

GO ⟩

ANSWER ROWS   E1 Ⓐ Ⓑ Ⓒ Ⓓ   2 Ⓕ Ⓖ Ⓗ Ⓙ   5 Ⓐ Ⓑ Ⓒ Ⓓ   8 Ⓕ Ⓖ Ⓗ Ⓙ
              E2 Ⓕ Ⓖ Ⓗ Ⓙ   3 Ⓐ Ⓑ Ⓒ Ⓓ   6 Ⓕ Ⓖ Ⓗ Ⓙ   9 Ⓐ Ⓑ Ⓒ Ⓓ
              1 Ⓐ Ⓑ Ⓒ Ⓓ   4 Ⓕ Ⓖ Ⓗ Ⓙ   7 Ⓐ Ⓑ Ⓒ Ⓓ   10 Ⓕ Ⓖ Ⓗ Ⓙ

83

For numbers 11-13, read each answer. Fill in the space for the choice that has a spelling error. If there is no mistake, fill in the last answer space.

11 A refreshed
    B history
    C appropreat
    D ordinary
    E *(No mistakes)*

12 F commercial
    G poster
    H scenery
    J convince
    K *(No mistakes)*

13 A success
    B appearance
    C fawlty
    D wages
    E *(No mistakes)*

For numbers 14-16, read each phrase. One of the underlined words is not spelled correctly for the way it is used in the phrase. Fill in the space for the word that is not spelled correctly.

14 F cheese <u>greater</u>
    G <u>react</u> quickly
    H <u>extra</u> cheese
    J hard <u>practice</u>

15 A can <u>trap</u> a mouse
    B have a better <u>idea</u>
    C <u>mean</u> what you say
    D will <u>except</u> the award

16 F grant your <u>wishes</u>
    G <u>chews</u> a book to read
    H <u>approve</u> of a decision
    J try to <u>explain</u> why

For numbers 17-20, find the underlined part that is misspelled. If all of the words are spelled correctly, mark the space under <u>No mistake</u>.

17 The baseball <u>championship</u> was <u>played</u> on <u>artifical</u> turf. <u>No mistake</u>.
                        A   B   C   D

18 She <u>earned</u> a <u>reputation</u> for being a <u>dedacated</u> student. <u>No mistake</u>.
            F   G   H   J

19 Your <u>salery</u> will <u>increase</u> the longer you remain <u>employed</u>. <u>No mistake</u>.
            A   B   C   D

20 Repairing the <u>pump</u> will be <u>unnecessary</u> if you <u>maintain</u> it well. <u>No mistake</u>.
                    F   G   H   J

ANSWER ROWS   11 Ⓐ Ⓑ Ⓒ Ⓓ Ⓔ   14 Ⓕ Ⓖ Ⓗ Ⓙ Ⓚ   17 Ⓐ Ⓑ Ⓒ Ⓓ Ⓔ   19 Ⓐ Ⓑ Ⓒ Ⓓ Ⓔ
              12 Ⓕ Ⓖ Ⓗ Ⓙ Ⓚ   15 Ⓐ Ⓑ Ⓒ Ⓓ Ⓔ   18 Ⓕ Ⓖ Ⓗ Ⓙ Ⓚ   20 Ⓕ Ⓖ Ⓗ Ⓙ Ⓚ
              13 Ⓐ Ⓑ Ⓒ Ⓓ Ⓔ   16 Ⓕ Ⓖ Ⓗ Ⓙ Ⓚ

84

NUMBER RIGHT _____

Lesson 10   Study Skills

Example   **Directions:** Follow the directions for each section. Choose the answer you think is correct.

Table of Contents		A	In which chapter would you find data about the population of your state?

Table of Contents

Chapter		Page
1	Awards	1
2	Census, 1990	9
3	Economics	16
4	Sports	24

A In which chapter would you find data about the population of your state?

A   1
B   2
C   3
D   4

Be sure to refer to any reference material or graphic that is part of the question.

After you have chosen the answer you think is correct, ask yourself: "Does this make sense?"

Practice

Use this section of a newspaper to answer numbers 1 and 2.

WEEKLY ALMANAC

INDEX	
The Arts	C1
Business & Money	B1
Classified	B4
Comics	C5
Crossword	C6
Local News	A2
Opinion & Editorial	A7
Weather	A3
World News	A4

Main Street Accident Injures Two

A three-car accident on Main Street yesterday sent two people to County Hospital. Millie Lintner and Warren Harris are both in good condition, according to a hospital spokesperson.

The accident occurred at 1:32 at the corner of Main and Howard Streets. Lintner and Harris were in their vehicles waiting for the light to change when a truck

Mayor Declines Fifth Term: "It's Been Fun, But Eight Years Is It."

In a long-awaited announcement, Mayor Miriam Kreitner indicated her intention not to run for a fifth term. "It's time for someone else to take over the office. I want to spend time with my grandchildren and get ten year's worth of weeds out of my garden."

1   Which section would you turn to if you wanted to learn more about a trip taken by the Queen of England?

A   Business & Money
B   Local News
C   Weather
D   World News

2   If you wanted to buy a used guitar, you would probably turn to page —

F   C1
G   B4
H   A2
J   A7

GO ⟩

In a library, the Dewey Decimal System is used to categorize nonfiction books. Use the summary of this system to do numbers 3-6.

000-099 Generalities (encyclopedias, periodicals)
100-199 Philosophy and Related Disciplines
200-299 Religion
300-399 Social Sciences (law, government)
400-499 Language
500-599 Pure Sciences (math, chemistry)
600-699 Technology (applied sciences, medicine)
700-799 The Arts and Recreation
800-899 Literature
900-999 Geography and History

3 The information in the parentheses shows just a few of the topics that are found under each main heading. Which of these topics would also be found under "Pure Sciences"?

A designing a house
B auto mechanics
C hunting
D physics

4 Where would a book about opera be categorized?

F 400-499   **H** 800-899
G 700-799   **J** 900-999

5 How would a book about conversational Spanish be categorized?

A 000-099   **C** 400-499
B 100-199   **D** 800-899

6 Which of these books would probably be found in category 800-899?

F *The Collected Works of Shakespeare*
G *The World's Great Religions*
H *The Encyclopedia of Woodworking*
J *Political Geography*

Read each question below. Mark the space for the answer you think is correct.

7 Look at these guide words from a dictionary page.

> bran–brought

Which word could be found on the page?

A brow   **C** bread
B bramble   **D** brush

8 Look at these guide words from a dictionary page.

> weary–weave

Which word could be found on the page?

F weasel   **H** wealthy
G weak   **J** week

9 Look at the list below. How is the list organized?

> desert
> tropic
> temperate
> arctic

A altitude
B population
C cloud structure
D climate

STOP

Examples   **Directions:** Read each question. Mark the space for the answer you think is correct.

E1

The first place to look to find magazine articles about the most popular travel destinations in the United States is —

A an atlas
B an encyclopedia
C the telephone directory
D the *Readers' Guide to Periodical Literature*

E2

In a research report, where would you find a list of the books the writer used?

F in the introduction
G in the bibliography
H in the body
J in the table of contents

Study the poster below. Use it to do numbers 1-4.

Do something for yourself this summer! Sign up for a continuing education class.

CENTRAL UNIVERSITY invites you to make it the best summer ever. With more than a hundred courses, we probably have something for you.

Computers	Swimming
Horseback Riding	Cartooning
Fishing	Guitar
Real Estate	Painting
Cooking	Photography

and much more

IMPORTANT DATES

Mail-in registration deadline	April 21
Walk-in registration deadline	April 28
Classes begin	June 15
Classes end	August 6

OFFICE HOURS
Main Campus
       Mon. – Fri., 8:00 AM – 5:00 PM
Suburban Campus
       Wed. – Sat., 1:00 PM – 9:00 PM

HOW TO ENROLL
Call 555-2728 for course information and an application form. Application forms are also available at most post offices in town. Completed forms may be faxed to 555-6341. Special arrangements for disabled students can be made by calling 555-1315. Group discounts (five or more people) are available by calling 555-4792.

WHO MAY ENROLL
· Most courses are available to those eighteen years and older. Those under eighteen may take courses in the Young People's College.

---

1 What number should a person who uses a wheelchair call to make arrangements to take a course?

A 555-4792
B 555-6341
C 555-2728
D 555-1315

2 When might be a good time to visit the office on the suburban campus?

F Monday at 7:00 PM
G Friday at 7:00 PM
H Friday at 10:00 AM
J Saturday at 10:00 AM

3 How might you obtain a lower price if you wanted to take a course?

A Find four friends to take the course with you.
B Send in your form before April 21.
C Prove that you are under 18 years of age.
D Send your form to the Suburban Campus office before 9:00 PM on Saturday.

4 Which information is not included on the poster?

F the date of the first class
G the date of the last class
H the cost of a course
J how to fax an application

GO >

Use the Table of Contents and Index below to answer numbers 5-9. They are from an automobile buyer's manual.

Table of Contents

Index

5 Information about the kind of soap you should use to wash the car would be found in chapter —

A   1
B   4
C   7
D   9

6 Which of these is not included in Chapter 7?

F   driving on ice
G   air bags
H   flashers for emergencies
J   controls

7 Which of these topics is probably included in Chapter 8 but does not appear in the index?

A   the first thing you should do when you want to drive your car
B   how you can adjust the brightness of the interior lights
C   where you can get your car serviced if there is a warranty problem
D   how to adjust the roof rack for long items like lumber or skis

8 From looking at the index, what can you conclude about this car?

F   The only indicators discussed in Chapter 3 are for battery, fuel, and temperature.
G   More than one type of engine is available.
H   It has air bags but not seat belts.
J   There is only one kind of tire you can use with the car.

9 Which of these is found in Chapter 6?

A   changing oil
B   fastening seat belts
C   waxing the car
D   how to set the trip odometer

GO

Katie is writing an essay comparing the architecture used in different places of the world throughout history. Keep this in mind when you do numbers 10 and 11.

10 What would be a good method for Katie to use to organize her essay?

 F compare noted buildings from the same time period but in one place, like Europe

 G examine the materials used for historic buildings throughout the United States

 H examine the methods people used to move large stones in Egypt, South America, and Asia

 J compare noted buildings from the same time period but in different places throughout the world

11 To begin her report, Katie wants to read general information about architecture and its history. Which of these should she use?

 A a book on world history

 B an encyclopedia

 C the biography of a famous architect

 D a thesaurus

For number 12, read the sentences below. Then choose the essential phrase that Katie should include in her notes about the history of architecture.

12 Builders in many places throughout the world have used the pyramid shape for constructing large buildings and memorials. They have also depended on available materials such as wood from nearby forests or stone from local quarries.

 F most pyramids made of wood or stone

 G large buildings and memorials; pyramids made of wood or stone

 H builders used pyramid shape; depended on available materials

 J builders in many places; pyramids; wood and stone

For numbers 13-15, choose the word that would appear first if the words were arranged in alphabetical order.

13 **A** noble
 B nobby
 C nobody
 D Nobel

14 **F** snare
 G snazzy
 H snarl
 J snatch

15 **A** claim
 B clang
 C clack
 D clap

For numbers 16 and 17, choose the answer you think is correct.

16 Which of these would you most likely find in the index of a history book?

 F solar power, 227-256

 G Manfred Publishing, San Francisco

 H cholla: a type of branched cactus

 J westward expansion, 145-173

17 Which of these books would be the best source of information for a report about changing fashions in clothing?

 A *Clothing through the Ages*

 B *Sewing Your Own Clothes*

 C *Dressing for Success*

 D *Your Guide to Careers in Fashion*

STOP

Name and Answer Sheet

To the Student:

These tests will give you a chance to put the tips you have learned to work.

A few last reminders…

- Be sure you understand all the directions before you begin each test. You may ask the teacher questions about the directions if you do not understand them.
- Work as quickly as you can during each test.
- When you change an answer, be sure to erase your first mark completely.

- You can guess at an answer or skip difficult items and go back to them later.
- Use the tips you have learned whenever you can.
- It is OK to be a little nervous. You may even do better.

Now that you have completed the lessons in this unit, you are on your way to scoring high!

STUDENT'S NAME		SCHOOL
LAST	FIRST	MI	TEACHER

FEMALE ○   MALE ○

BIRTHDATE

MONTH	DAY	YEAR

JAN ○
FEB ○
MAR ○
APR ○
MAY ○
JUN ○
JUL ○
AUG ○
SEP ○
OCT ○
NOV ○
DEC ○

GRADE
⑥ ⑦ ⑧

PART 1   LANGUAGE MECHANICS

E1 Ⓐ Ⓑ Ⓒ Ⓓ	4 Ⓕ Ⓖ Ⓗ Ⓙ	8 Ⓕ Ⓖ Ⓗ Ⓙ	12 Ⓕ Ⓖ Ⓗ Ⓙ	16 Ⓕ Ⓖ Ⓗ Ⓙ	19 Ⓐ Ⓑ Ⓒ Ⓓ
1 Ⓐ Ⓑ Ⓒ Ⓓ	5 Ⓐ Ⓑ Ⓒ Ⓓ	9 Ⓐ Ⓑ Ⓒ Ⓓ	13 Ⓐ Ⓑ Ⓒ Ⓓ	17 Ⓐ Ⓑ Ⓒ Ⓓ	20 Ⓕ Ⓖ Ⓗ Ⓙ
2 Ⓕ Ⓖ Ⓗ Ⓙ	6 Ⓕ Ⓖ Ⓗ Ⓙ	10 Ⓕ Ⓖ Ⓗ Ⓙ	14 Ⓕ Ⓖ Ⓗ Ⓙ	18 Ⓕ Ⓖ Ⓗ Ⓙ	21 Ⓐ Ⓑ Ⓒ Ⓓ
3 Ⓐ Ⓑ Ⓒ Ⓓ	7 Ⓐ Ⓑ Ⓒ Ⓓ	11 Ⓐ Ⓑ Ⓒ Ⓓ	15 Ⓐ Ⓑ Ⓒ Ⓓ		

PART 2   LANGUAGE EXPRESSION

E1 Ⓐ Ⓑ Ⓒ Ⓓ	4 Ⓕ Ⓖ Ⓗ Ⓙ	8 Ⓕ Ⓖ Ⓗ Ⓙ	12 Ⓕ Ⓖ Ⓗ Ⓙ	15 Ⓐ Ⓑ Ⓒ Ⓓ	18 Ⓕ Ⓖ Ⓗ Ⓙ
1 Ⓐ Ⓑ Ⓒ Ⓓ	5 Ⓐ Ⓑ Ⓒ Ⓓ	9 Ⓐ Ⓑ Ⓒ Ⓓ	13 Ⓐ Ⓑ Ⓒ Ⓓ	16 Ⓕ Ⓖ Ⓗ Ⓙ	19 Ⓐ Ⓑ Ⓒ Ⓓ
2 Ⓕ Ⓖ Ⓗ Ⓙ	6 Ⓕ Ⓖ Ⓗ Ⓙ	10 Ⓕ Ⓖ Ⓗ Ⓙ	14 Ⓕ Ⓖ Ⓗ Ⓙ	17 Ⓐ Ⓑ Ⓒ Ⓓ	20 Ⓕ Ⓖ Ⓗ Ⓙ
3 Ⓐ Ⓑ Ⓒ Ⓓ	7 Ⓐ Ⓑ Ⓒ Ⓓ	11 Ⓐ Ⓑ Ⓒ Ⓓ			

PART 3   SPELLING

E1 Ⓐ Ⓑ Ⓒ Ⓓ	3 Ⓐ Ⓑ Ⓒ Ⓓ	7 Ⓐ Ⓑ Ⓒ Ⓓ	11 Ⓐ Ⓑ Ⓒ Ⓓ	15 Ⓐ Ⓑ Ⓒ Ⓓ	19 Ⓐ Ⓑ Ⓒ Ⓓ
E2 Ⓕ Ⓖ Ⓗ Ⓙ	4 Ⓕ Ⓖ Ⓗ Ⓙ	8 Ⓕ Ⓖ Ⓗ Ⓙ	12 Ⓕ Ⓖ Ⓗ Ⓙ	16 Ⓕ Ⓖ Ⓗ Ⓙ	20 Ⓕ Ⓖ Ⓗ Ⓙ
1 Ⓐ Ⓑ Ⓒ Ⓓ	5 Ⓐ Ⓑ Ⓒ Ⓓ	9 Ⓐ Ⓑ Ⓒ Ⓓ	13 Ⓐ Ⓑ Ⓒ Ⓓ	17 Ⓐ Ⓑ Ⓒ Ⓓ	
2 Ⓕ Ⓖ Ⓗ Ⓙ	6 Ⓕ Ⓖ Ⓗ Ⓙ	10 Ⓕ Ⓖ Ⓗ Ⓙ	14 Ⓕ Ⓖ Ⓗ Ⓙ	18 Ⓕ Ⓖ Ⓗ Ⓙ	

PART 4   STUDY SKILLS

E1 Ⓐ Ⓑ Ⓒ Ⓓ	3 Ⓐ Ⓑ Ⓒ Ⓓ	6 Ⓕ Ⓖ Ⓗ Ⓙ	9 Ⓐ Ⓑ Ⓒ Ⓓ
1 Ⓐ Ⓑ Ⓒ Ⓓ	4 Ⓕ Ⓖ Ⓗ Ⓙ	7 Ⓐ Ⓑ Ⓒ Ⓓ	10 Ⓕ Ⓖ Ⓗ Ⓙ
2 Ⓕ Ⓖ Ⓗ Ⓙ	5 Ⓐ Ⓑ Ⓒ Ⓓ	8 Ⓕ Ⓖ Ⓗ Ⓙ	11 Ⓐ Ⓑ Ⓒ Ⓓ

Part 1   Language Mechanics

Example   **Directions:** Fill in the answer circle for the punctuation mark that is needed in the sentence. Choose "None" if no more punctuation is needed in the sentence.

E1

Do you know what time it is?

A .   B ;   C ,   D None

---

1   Several students won awards at the science fair: Lorraine Edie, and Samuel.

A .   B ,   C ;   D None

2   "The item you are looking for is out of stock, answered the clerk.

F "   G .   H !   J None

3   The moon was full and we could clearly see the boats on the lake.

A :   B ,   C ;   D None

4   No, you are still too sick to play outside.

F ,   G ?   H :   J None

For numbers 5-7, read each answer. Fill in the space for the choice that has a punctuation error. If there is no mistake, fill in the fourth answer space.

5   A   Alida went jogging
       B   around the lake in the park
       C   with Pookie her dog.
       D   *(No mistakes)*

6   F   "Look at that huge
       G   tree!" shouted Max. "It's the
       H   biggest one I've ever seen."
       J   *(No mistakes)*

7   A   If the road's are covered
       B   with snow, it will take us
       C   longer to get to Tad's house.
       D   *(No mistakes)*

For numbers 8 and 9, read each sentence with a blank. Choose the word or words that fit best in the blank and show the correct punctuation.

8   This map shows all the rivers and hiking trails in the _____ Tracy

       F   state
       G   state;
       H   state:
       J   state,

9   All the _____ cars should be parked in the lot near the gymnasium.

       A   visitors
       B   visitors'
       C   visitor's
       D   visitors's

GO

For numbers 10-12, read each answer. Fill in the space for the choice that has a capitalization error. If there is no mistake, fill in the fourth answer space.

10 **F**   The wind filled the sails of
    G   the ships in the Harbor, and
    H   the starter fired her cannon.
    J   *(No mistakes)*

11 **A**   The tunnel between england
    B   and France was completed
    C   in 1994 after many years of work.
    D   *(No mistakes)*

12 **F**   The Gulf of Mexico provides
    G   recreation for people living
    H   in many of the southern states.
    J   *(No mistakes)*

For number 13, read each answer choice. Find the one that is written correctly and shows the correct capitalization and punctuation.

13 **A**   "This is the easiest part of the climb." remarked Diana. "Its pretty flat and there are trees to shade us. We should try to make good time here."

    B   Paul looked at the steep slope and muttered, "we'll have to take this section slowly. It isnt dangerous, but it will be a lot of work."

    C   "Whats this, wondered Daphne." It looks like a clam shell stuck in a rock. Maybe it's a fossil. My teacher said this part of the state used to be under water.

    D   "I'm really tired," said Palmer. "Can't we take a break now? If we rest for about ten minutes, I'm sure I can finish up without stopping."

For numbers 14-16, read the sentence with a blank. Mark the space beside the answer choice that fits best in the blank and has correct capitalization and punctuation.

14 The chain saw is in the _____ you must be very careful when you use it.

    F   garage, but
    G   garage: But
    H   garage but
    J   garage; but

15 Texas has a huge _____ is completely landlocked.

    A   Coastline: Oklahoma
    B   coastline, Oklahoma
    C   Coastline. oklahoma
    D   coastline; Oklahoma

16 During the summer vacation, my family hopes to go _____ .

    F   horseback riding, hiking, and biking
    G   horseback, riding, hiking, and biking
    H   horseback riding hiking, and biking
    J   horseback riding hiking and biking

Choose the correct answer for number 17.

17 Which is the correct way to begin a business letter?

    A   Dear Dr. Lincoln
    B   Dear Dr. Lincoln,
    C   Dear Dr. Lincoln:
    D   Dear Dr. Lincoln;

Part 1   Language Mechanics

Adrian is describing her town to a pen pal who lives in Spain. Read her description and use it to do numbers 18-21.

The name of the city in which I live is
(1)
Columbus. It is the capital of the <u>state of ohio</u>
(2)
and is located near the center of the state.

More than a million people live in Columbus and
(3)
<u>it's surrounding</u> area.

Although it is a large city, Columbus has the
(4)
feel of a small town. There are only a few
(5)
skyscrapers in the center of town, and most of the

city is made up of pleasant residential areas. We
(6)
have many <u>parks, playgrounds, and recreation</u> areas

in the city and suburbs.

The <u>Ohio State university</u> is located in
(7)
Columbus. It is really large, with more than 60,000
(8)
students. The university is most well-known for its
(9)
football team. People here are crazy about it.
(10)

---

18 In sentence 2, <u>state of ohio</u> is best written —

  F State of Ohio
  G state of Ohio
  H state, of Ohio
  J As it is

19 In sentence 3, <u>it's surrounding</u> is best written —

  A its surrounding
  B its' surrounding
  C its, surrounding
  D As it is

20 In sentence 6, <u>parks, playgrounds, and recreation</u> is best written —

  F parks, playgrounds, and recreation,
  G parks playgrounds and recreation
  H parks, playgrounds, and, recreation
  J As it is

21 In sentence 7, <u>Ohio State university</u> is best written —

  A Ohio state University
  B Ohio state university
  C Ohio State University
  D As it is

STOP

Example   Directions: Find the underlined part that is the simple predicate (verb) of the sentence.

E1

   The <u>mail</u> <u>carrier</u> <u>usually</u> <u>arrives</u> between ten and eleven o'clock.
            A   B   C   D

For number 1, choose the word or phrase that best completes the sentence.

1   Todd's dog waited _____ for him outside the store.

   A more patient

   B patient

   C patiently

   D patienter

For number 2, choose the answer that is a complete and correctly written sentence.

2   **F** Nora and me took a train ride through New England.

   G Be sure you give yourself enough time to reach the airport.

   H The ship's captain gave Larry and I a tour of the engine room.

   J We found themselves waiting in the rain for a taxi cab.

For numbers 3-5, read each answer choice. Fill in the space for the choice that has a usage error. If there is no mistake, fill in the fourth answer space.

3   **A**   An exciting basketball game
      B will be held in the school's
      C gymnasium on Friday night.
      D *(No mistakes)*

4   **F**   There wasn't nothing wrong with
      G Johnson, but he went to the
      H doctor for his regular checkup.
      J *(No mistakes)*

5   **A**   My grandfather is in such good
      B shape that most people think he is
      C more younger than he really is.
      D *(No mistakes)*

For number 6, find the underlined part that is the simple subject of the sentence.

6   <u>Next week</u>, the <u>highway</u> will be <u>closed</u> for repairs.
    F **G**   **H**   **J**

For number 7, find the underlined part that is the simple predicate (verb) of the sentence.

7   A <u>group</u> of <u>foreign</u> tourists <u>enjoyed</u> their <u>visit</u> to our town.
      A   **B**   **C**   **D**

GO

For numbers 8-10, choose the answer that best combines the underlined sentences.

8 Mr. Alston seems very gruff.

Mr. Alston is actually a nice person with a great sense of humor.

    F Mr. Alston seems very gruff because he is actually a nice person with a great sense of humor.

    G Mr. Alston, who seems very gruff, yet he is actually a nice person with a great sense of humor.

    H Mr. Alston seems very gruff, or he is actually a nice person with a great sense of humor.

    J Mr. Alston seems very gruff, but he is actually a nice person with a great sense of humor.

9 Karen has just entered high school.

Karen is the state tennis champion.

    A Because Karen has just entered high school, she is the state tennis champion.

    B Karen, the state tennis champion, who has just entered high school.

    C Karen, who has just entered high school, is the state tennis champion.

    D The state tennis champion who has just entered high school is Karen.

10 The bird feeder is near the fence.

Some seeds spilled on the ground.

The seeds are beginning to sprout.

    F Some seeds from the bird feeder near the fence spilled on the ground and are beginning to sprout.

    G From the bird feeder near the fence and some seeds spilled on the ground and are beginning to sprout.

    H The bird feeder near the fence, which spilled some sprouting seeds on the ground.

    J On the ground are some spilled, sprouting seeds from the bird feeder near the fence.

For numbers 11 and 12, choose the best way of expressing the idea.

11 **A** In the bank is the money I have for my college education.
     B The money I have in the bank is for my college education.
     C For my college education, I have money in the bank.
     D The money, that I have for my college education, is in the bank.

12 **F** Our local hospital is where Rhonda volunteers as the president of our class.
     G The president of our class, who is Rhonda, is a volunteer at our local hospital.
     H Rhonda, who is a volunteer at our local hospital, although she is our class president.
     J Rhonda, the president of our class, is a volunteer at our local hospital.

GO

Read the paragraph below. Find the best topic sentence for the paragraph.

13 _____ . Constructed of more than two million blocks of stone, the Great Pyramid covers about thirteen acres. Completing the pyramid took more than twenty years, and scientists are still not sure how it was built.

    A Egypt holds many mysteries, including the construction of the pyramids.

    B The Great Pyramid of Khufu is a remarkable monument.

    C The Great Pyramid of Khufu and the Sphinx are in Egypt.

    D The ancient Egyptians were able to build remarkable monuments.

Find the answer choice that best develops the topic sentence.

14 Americans who earn a salary pay an income tax to the federal government.

    F Each pay period, part of what they earned is withheld and sent to the government. This money is used for a variety of purposes, such as maintaining the armed forces.

    G In most states, if you buy something you pay a sales tax. Even some cities have sales taxes.

    H Many states also have income taxes. For the federal income tax, the more you earn, the higher the tax rate you pay.

    J Tax day is April 15, a day many people dread. Post offices around the country stay open late so people can get their taxes in on time.

Read the paragraph below. Find the sentence that does not belong in the paragraph.

15 1. Thomas Hopkins Gallaudet, born in 1787, traveled to France to learn how to teach deaf people.   2. He returned to the United States and opened a school for deaf people in 1817.   3. Gallaudet's health was never very good.   4. T.H. Gallaudet's son, Edward, followed in his father's footsteps and founded what is now known as Gallaudet University.

    A Sentence 1

    B Sentence 2

    C Sentence 3

    D Sentence 4

Read the paragraph below. Find the sentence that best fits the blank in the paragraph.

16   Lydia never thought of herself as a hero. _____. A little girl fell into the river and was swept away by the current. Without thinking twice, Lydia jumped into the river and rescued the girl. Now she was a national celebrity whose story was on the news.

    F She enjoyed many sports, especially swimming.

    G She was a good student and made friends easily.

    H After all, she was just thirteen years old, and had never had an adventure.

    J An incident at Walker River State Park changed all that, however.

GO >

Below is more of Adrian's description of her town for a pen pal who lives in Spain. Read the story and use it to do numbers 17-20.

Two rivers flow through Columbus. The rivers are
(1)   **(2)**
the Sciota and the Olentangy. Both rivers are too
(3)
small for commercial shipping, but they are used

often for recreation. There is a dam on the Sciota
(4)
River, and it has formed a lake. The lake is used
(5)
for fishing and boating, especially water skiing.

Many different businesses are in Columbus. They
(6)   **(7)**
<u>include</u> insurance companies, publishing companies,

and chemical companies. Ohio is also an
(8)
agricultural state with many large and small farms.

Columbus has a unique distinction: it is a test
(9)
market city. This means that many businesses try
(10)
out their products or services in Columbus before

they move to other areas of the country.

17 **How would sentences 1 and 2 best be combined without changing their meaning?**

A Because two rivers flow through Columbus, they are the Sciota and the Olentangy.
B Two rivers flow through Columbus, the Sciota and the Olentangy.
C The Sciota and the Olentangy, which are the two rivers that flow through Columbus.
D Two rivers, which flow through Columbus, the Sciota and the Olentangy.

18 **Which of these sentences does not belong in this report?**

F 5
G 6
H 8
J 9

19 **How is sentence 4 best written?**

A There is a dam on the Sciota River that has formed a lake.
B On the Sciota River is a lake, which has been formed by a dam.
C A dam, on the Sciota River, which has formed a lake.
D As it is

20 **In sentence 7, <u>include</u> is best written —**

F included
G will include
H including
J As it is

STOP

Examples   Directions: For E1, mark the answer circle for the word that is spelled correctly and fits best in the sentence. For E2, choose the underlined word that has a spelling mistake.

E1

The medicine was _____ .

A afective
B efective
C effective
D effectave

E2

F detour around

G true belief

H sick patiunt

J withdraw money

For numbers 1-6, find the word that is spelled correctly and fits best in the blank.

1 What was the _____ of the trial?

A verdick
B verdect
C verdict
D verduct

2 The landscape was _____ and empty.

F bleke
G bliek
H bleek
J bleak

3 The teacher will _____ the students.

A praise
B prais
C prayse
D priase

4 The children enjoyed the _____ music.

F livly
G livelly
H liveley
J lively

5 Mandy and Chris joined an _____ to South America.

A expidition
B expadition
C expedition
D expeditition

6 The road makes a _____ turn here.

F dangerus
G dangourous
H dangerous
J dangurous

For numbers 7-10, read the phrases. Choose the phrase in which the underlined word is not spelled correctly.

7 A enjoyable hobby

    B earn intrest

    C civil service

    D juicy apple

8 F scientific analysas

    G openly worried

    H long process

    J emerge quickly

9 A protect people

    B elementary school

    C soon reapear

    D become angry

10 F hot sidewalk

    G feel helpless

    H clumsy action

    J entertane friends

GO

For numbers 11-13, read each answer. Fill in the space for the choice that has a spelling error. If there is no mistake, fill in the last answer space.

11 A offended
    B unused
    C reckless
    D consistant
    E *(No mistakes)*

12 F strategy
    G advice
    H deceive
    J language
    K *(No mistakes)*

13 A vanish
    B edible
    C multaply
    D generous
    E *(No mistakes)*

For numbers 14-16, read each phrase. One of the underlined words is not spelled correctly for the way it is used in the phrase. Fill in the space for the word that is not spelled correctly.

14 F narrow <u>passage</u>
    G fish <u>scale</u>
    H <u>forth</u> in line
    J <u>control</u> a plane

15 A toll <u>booth</u>
    B loud <u>grown</u>
    C dull <u>party</u>
    D <u>mild</u> weather

16 F beautiful <u>seen</u>
    G large <u>reward</u>
    H <u>slide</u> down
    J <u>fair</u> rules

For numbers 17-20, find the underlined part that is misspelled. If all of the words are spelled correctly, mark the space under <u>No mistake</u>.

17 We <u>stumbled</u> upon the <u>ideal</u> <u>site</u> to set up camp. <u>No mistake.</u>
        A   B C   D

18 Katrina <u>served</u> as an <u>obzerver</u> during the school <u>elections</u>. <u>No mistake.</u>
          F   G   H   J

19 Vincent <u>completed</u> a <u>lingthy</u> essay about <u>preparing</u> healthful meals. <u>No mistake.</u>
          A   B   C   D

20 One <u>competator</u> was <u>injured</u> <u>slightly</u> in the game. <u>No mistake.</u>
          F   G H   J

STOP

Example   Directions: Read the outline. Mark the space for the answer you think is correct.

OUTLINE

Identifying Rocks
1. Color
2. Texture
3. Location Where Found
4. _____
5. Shape

E1

Which of these would fit best on Line 4 of the outline on the left?

A Weather When Found
B Density
C Jewelry Type
D Altitude

Use this card from a library card catalog to do numbers 1-3.

611.34

B   **Barton, Henry**
Gardening All Year / Henry Barton; photographs and charts by Phoebe Miller. Foreword by Sandy McGill. Miami: Southern Shores Publishing Company, 1994.
256 pages; photos and charts; 25 cm (The Home Improvement series, vol. 2)

1. Gardening   2. Home gardening
3. Hobbies   I. Title

---

1 Which guide letters indicate the card catalog drawer in which this card would be found?

A Hab–Hol
B Bea–Bri
C Are–Bal
D Bai–Ble

2 What other book might be part of the same series as this book?

F *Home Carpentry*
G *Electrical Engineering*
H *Planning a Career*
J *Cooking for Two*

3 In which section of the card catalog would this card be found?

A Title
B Subject
C Publisher
D Author

Choose the best answer for numbers 4-7.

4 Which of these might you find in a thesaurus?

F a quotation by Margaret Mead
G a synonym for the word *unstable*
H the population of Indonesia
J a list of recent magazine articles

5 Definitions of the terms used in a physics textbook would be found in —

A the glossary
B the index
C the table of contents
D the bibliography

6 Under which of these encyclopedia entries would you find information about how the stock market and consumer buying patterns affect the economy?

F Consumers
G Stock Market
H Economics
J Investing

7 Which of these topics would be specific enough for you to write a report that was only two pages long?

A science
B feathers
C living things
D the history of science

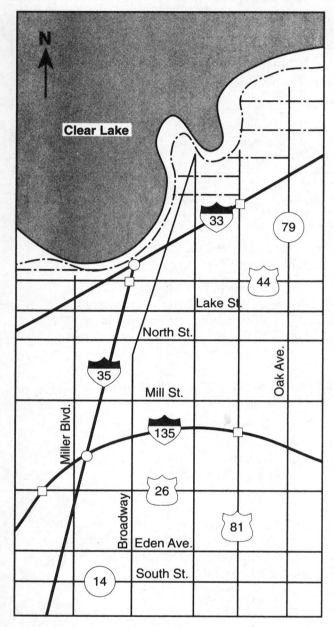

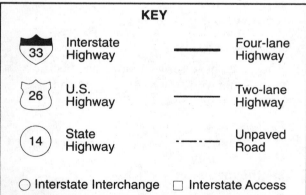

KEY

🛡️ 33	Interstate Highway	———	Four-lane Highway
⬡ 26	U.S. Highway	———	Two-lane Highway
◯ 14	State Highway	–··–··–	Unpaved Road

◯ Interstate Interchange   ☐ Interstate Access

Use the map on the left to do numbers 8-11.

8 South St. is also —

   F State Highway 14
   G U.S. Highway 14
   H U.S. Highway 26
   J State Highway 79

9 It is two miles from the interchange of Interstates 35 and 33 to the access where U.S. 81 enters Interstate 33. About how far is it from Broadway to U.S. 81?

   A exactly two miles
   B more than two miles
   C less than two miles
   D It cannot be determined.

10 Using this map, which of these statements is true?

   F The only access to an interstate highway is through another interstate.
   G Access can be gained to an interstate highway through state highways.
   H Unpaved roads are found on the south shore of the lake.
   J Unpaved roads are found on the north shore of the lake.

11 Suppose you left Interstate 135 at U.S. Route 81. Which direction should you travel to reach the corner of Lake St. and Miller Boulevard?

   A north on U.S. 81, west on Mill St. and south on Miller Blvd.
   B north on U.S. 81 and west on Lake St.
   C south on U.S. 81 and west on Miller Blvd.
   D south on U.S. 81, west on Eden Ave. and north on Broadway

STOP

Table of Contents
Math

Lesson 1   Numeration

Example   **Directions:** Read and work each problem. Find the correct answer.
Mark the space for your choice.

A Which of these numbers is a common
multiple of 2, 3, and 9?

   A 45

   B 39

   C 22

   D 18

B Which of these is smaller than $^-2$?

   F 0

   G $^-1$

   H $^-3$

   J 2

Read each question carefully. Look for key words and numbers that will help you find the answers.

Be sure the answer circle you fill in is the same letter as the answer you think is correct.

Practice

1 Which point is at $\frac{3}{4}$ on this number line?

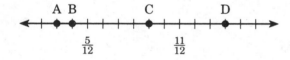

   A A

   B B

   C C

   D D

2 Which of these is another way to write the
number in the box?

$$22{,}000{,}000 + 300{,}000 + 80 + 1$$

   F 223,801

   G 22,300,081

   H 25,000,081

   J 25,000,801

3 What number is expressed by

$$(4 \times 10^3) + (1 \times 10^2) + (6 \times 10^1)$$

   A 4160

   B 416

   C 41,600

   D 400,106

4 $\sqrt{81}$ =

   F 6

   G 7

   H 8

   J 9

5 Which of these is less than 10^2?

   A 100

   B 95

   C 110

   D 130

ANSWER ROWS   A ⒶⒷ©Ⓓ   1 ⒶⒷ©Ⓓ   3 ⒶⒷ©Ⓓ   5 ⒶⒷ©Ⓓ
                B ⒻⒼⒽⒿ   2 ⒻⒼⒽⒿ   4 ⒻⒼⒽⒿ

6 Which of these is between 0.01 and 0.1 in value?

   F 0.2

   G 0.009

   H 0.6

   J 0.07

7 What is the value of the expression in the box?

$$9 - 2 \times 4 =$$

   A 17

   B $^{-}1$

   C 1

   D 28

8 $2.3 \times 10^3 =$

   F   2300

   G   23,000

   H 2,300,000

   J   230

9 $^{-}9 + 12 =$

   A $^{-}3$

   B 3

   C 21

   D $^{-}21$

10 What is the *least* number that can be divided evenly by 9 and 12?

   F 72

   G 108

   H 36

   J 18

11 Which of these is another name for 5^3?

   A 5×3

   B $3 \times 3 \times 3 \times 3 \times 3$

   C $5 \times 5 \times 5$

   D 2

12 What is the prime factorization of 54?

   F 4×9

   G $2 \times 3 \times 3 \times 3$

   H 3×6

   J $2 \times 2 \times 2 \times 2 \times 2$

13 Which of these is the greatest common factor of 24 and 60?

   A 12

   B 6

   C 10

   D 14

14 A mechanic needed some nuts and bolts. When he went to the store, he found that nuts were sold in 4-packs and bolts were sold in 6-packs. What is the smallest number of packs he can buy to get the same number of nuts and bolts?

   F 6 packs of nuts and 4 packs of bolts

   G 2 packs of nuts and 2 packs of bolts

   H 3 packs of nuts and 2 packs of bolts

   J 2 packs of nuts and 3 packs of bolts

15 How much must you add to $^{-}4$ to get a number greater than 10?

   A a number between 6 and 10

   B a number less than 6

   C a number less than $^{-}14$

   D a number greater than 14

STOP

Example   **Directions:** Read and work each problem. Find the correct answer. Mark the space for your choice.

A How would you read 12.8?	**B** Which of these is a composite number?
A twelve and eight tenths	**F** 19
B one hundred twenty eight	**G** 7
C twelve and eight hundredths	**H** 13
D one and twenty-eight hundredths	**J** 18

Be sure the answer space you fill in is the same number or letter as the answer you think is correct.

Key words, numbers, pictures, and figures will help you find the answers.

Practice

1 Which period is underlined in the numeral 32,981,274?

   A thousands
   B tens of thousands
   C hundreds of thousands
   D millions

2 What is 0.47 rounded to the nearest tenth?

   F 0.410
   G 0.45
   H 0.4
   J 0.5

3 What number goes in the box to make the number sentence true?

$$5 \times (2 + 9) = (5 \times 2) + (\square \times 9)$$

   A 5
   B 0
   C 4
   D 2

4 492.82 x 23.56 is closest to —

   F 1000
   G 10,000
   H 15,000
   J 1500

5 Look carefully at the number pattern below. Which of these number sentences could be used to find the number that is missing from the number pattern?

3, 4, 6, 9, 13, 18, 24, 31, 39, ___, 58

   A 58 - 9 = 51
   B 39 + 8 = 47
   C 39 + 9 = 48
   D 58 - 11 = 47

GO

6 Which of these is another way to write the number shown in the box?

$$200 + 30 + 0.7 + 0.02$$

F   23.72
G   237.2
H   203.072
J   230.72

7 What number completes this number sentence?

$$8 \times 30 = 10 \times \square$$

A   32
B   24
C   28
D   42

8 Which of these is not a prime number?

F   19
G   23
H   27
J   31

9 Which letters should appear in the last box in the pattern below?

A   O, P, Q, R
B   R, S, T, U
C   O, N, M, L
D   R, P, O, N

10 What should replace the box in the equation below?

$$2\tfrac{2}{3} + \dfrac{\square}{9} = 3\tfrac{2}{9}$$

F   11
G   2
H   5
J   1

11 How much would the value of 836,201 be increased by changing the 3 to an 8?

A   38,000
B   5000
C   50,000
D   80,000

12 Eight million, four hundred nine =

F   8,000,409
G   8,409,000
H   800,409
J   849,000

13 Look at the group of numbers in the box. Which statement about the numbers is true?

$$17, 25, 44, 59, 61$$

A All of them are prime numbers.
B All of the numbers are odd.
C None of the numbers are even.
D None of the numbers can be divided by 3.

STOP

ANSWER ROWS   6 Ⓕ Ⓖ Ⓗ Ⓙ   8 Ⓕ Ⓖ Ⓗ Ⓙ   10 Ⓕ Ⓖ Ⓗ Ⓙ   12 Ⓕ Ⓖ Ⓗ Ⓙ
              7 Ⓐ Ⓑ Ⓒ Ⓓ   9 Ⓐ Ⓑ Ⓒ Ⓓ   11 Ⓐ Ⓑ Ⓒ Ⓓ   13 Ⓐ Ⓑ Ⓒ Ⓓ

Example **Directions:** Read and work each problem. Find the correct answer. Mark the space for your choice.

A Which of these is larger than 7?

A $\frac{15}{2}$

B $\frac{2}{15}$

C $\frac{7}{1}$

D $\frac{1}{7}$

B Which decimal is another name for 51%?

F 0.051

G 5.1

H 0.51

J 5.01

Pay close attention to the numbers in the problem and in the answer choices. If you misread even one number, you will probably choose the wrong answer.

If you are sure you know which answer choice is correct, just fill in the space and move on to the next problem.

Practice

1 How much of this figure is shaded?

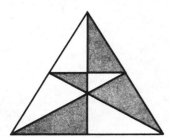

A $\frac{4}{9}$

B $\frac{5}{8}$

C $\frac{1}{3}$

D $\frac{1}{2}$

2 Which of these is less than 1.08?

F 1.16

G 1.27

H 1.027

J 1.09

3 What fraction is missing from the number pattern below?

$$\frac{2}{9}, \frac{1}{3}, \frac{4}{9}, \frac{5}{9}, \underline{\quad}, \frac{7}{9}$$

A $\frac{8}{3}$

B $\frac{2}{3}$

C $\frac{6}{7}$

D $\frac{7}{8}$

4 Which of these is forty-four and twenty-eight hundredths?

F 44.28

G 44.208

H 44.028

J 4428

GO

5 Which of these is <u>not</u> another way to write the number 0.75?

  A 0.75%

  B $\frac{9}{12}$

  C 75%

  D $\frac{3}{4}$

6 What is the simplest name for $\frac{12}{48}$?

  F $\frac{6}{22}$

  G $\frac{9}{14}$

  H $\frac{1}{4}$

  J $\frac{1}{2}$

7 What is the least common denominator for

  $\frac{1}{4}$, $\frac{2}{3}$, and $\frac{5}{9}$?

  A 12

  B 24

  C 72

  D 36

8 What is 92% expressed as a fraction?

  F $\frac{9}{2}$

  G $\frac{92}{100}$

  H $\frac{2}{9}$

  J $\frac{9}{200}$

9 What number must you add to $\frac{3}{4}$ to get a

  number that is greater than $2\frac{1}{2}$?

  A A number equal to $1\frac{1}{2}$

  B A number greater than $1\frac{1}{2}$

  C A number between 1 and $1\frac{1}{4}$

  D A number less than $1\frac{1}{2}$

10 Which of these is not equal in value to the others?

  F $\frac{6}{10}$

  G 60%

  H 20 ÷ 3

  J 0.6

11 Which of these percentages is closest in value to the portion of the circle that is shaded?

  A 90%

  B 30%

  C 10%

  D 50%

12 How many of the smaller figures will be needed to fill in the unshaded portion of this figure?

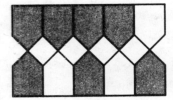

  F 10

  G 7

  H 3

  J 4

ANSWER ROWS **5** Ⓐ Ⓑ Ⓒ Ⓓ   **7** Ⓐ Ⓑ Ⓒ Ⓓ   **9** Ⓐ Ⓑ Ⓒ Ⓓ   **11** Ⓐ Ⓑ Ⓒ Ⓔ
  6 Ⓕ Ⓖ Ⓗ Ⓙ   **8** Ⓕ Ⓖ Ⓗ Ⓙ   **10** Ⓕ Ⓖ Ⓗ Ⓙ   **12** Ⓕ Ⓖ Ⓗ Ⓙ

109

Examples   **Directions:** Read each problem. Find the correct answer. Mark the space for your choice.

E1

Which of these is a common multiple of 2, 5, and 6?

A 45

B 24

C 30

D 12

E2

Which of these is another way to write the decimal 0.49?

F   4.9%

G   0.049%

H 490%

J   49%

---

1 Which of these is the greatest?

A sixteen tenths

B two hundred sixteen thousandths

C two and sixteen thousandths

D two and six tenths

2 Which expression is not the same as 4 x (8 + 2)?

F 4 x (2 + 8)

G (4 x 2) + (4 x 8)

H (4 x 8) + (4 x 2)

J (4 x 8) + 2

3 Which group of numbers includes 6, 8, 9, and 15?

A the composite numbers

B the prime numbers

C the factors of 30

D the multiples of 3

4 Which fraction is another name for $\frac{3}{8}$?

F $\frac{1}{4}$

G $\frac{9}{24}$

H $\frac{12}{36}$

J $\frac{12}{48}$

5 What is 282,971 rounded to the nearest hundred thousand?

A 300,000

B 200,000

C 280,000

D 283,000

6 If this pattern was continued, how many circles would be shaded in the last figure?

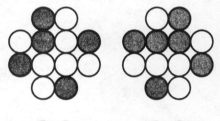

F 9

G 6

H 8

J 4

GO

7 In which of these problems can the dividend be evenly divided by its divisor?

   A $81 \div 6$

   B $83 \div 3$

   C $97 \div 7$

   D $98 \div 7$

8 What number is 100 more than 948,012?

   F 100,948,012

   G   949,012

   H 1,048,112

   J   948,112

9 What number completes this number sentence?

$$\square \times 9 = 30 \times 30$$

   A 100

   B 10

   C 21

   D 321

10 Arrow B points to which value on this number line?

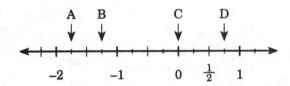

   F $-1\frac{1}{4}$

   G $1\frac{1}{4}$

   H $\frac{1}{4}$

   J $-2\frac{3}{4}$

11 3 thousands, 9 hundreds, and 8 hundred thousands equals —

   A   80,390

   B   39,800

   C 803,900

   D   83,900

12 $\frac{8}{15} = \frac{24}{\square}$ $\square =$

   F 60

   G 45

   H 30

   J 23

13 Which is between 1.47 and 1.93?

   A 1.43

   B 1.34

   C 1.74

   D 1.97

14 $216 =$

   F 16^2

   G 6^3

   H 4^3

   J 6^4

15 What number is expressed by

$$(2 \times 10^4) + (1 \times 10^3) + (9 \times 10^2) + (8 \times 10^1)$$

   A 21,980

   B 21,908

   C   2198

   D 219,008

STOP

Lesson 5   Addition

Example

Directions: Mark the space for the correct answer to each addition problem. Choose "None of these" if the right answer is not given.

A		A 175
		B 399
217		C 299
+ 182		D 75
		E None of these

B		F 13
		G 0
⁻4 + 9 =		H ⁻5
		J 4
		K None of these

Tips

If the right answer is not given, mark the space for "None of these."

Use rounding and estimation to get an idea of how large the correct answer should be. This will help you eliminate answer choices that are too large or too small.

Practice

1   0.029 + 0.097 =
A 0.026
B 0.116
C 0.0126
D 0.2997
E None of these

5   729.28
+ 73.552
A 702.333
B 655.728
C 802.333
D 802.832
E None of these

2   6.07
+ 2.9
F 4.2
G 3.17
H 8.79
J 8.97
K None of these

6   2.8 + 9.4 + 6.3 =
F 9.5
G 15.8
H 18.5
J 15.7
K None of these

3   6396
71
274
+ 2010
A 8751
B 8680
C 8741
D 6741
E None of these

7   1818
2
9176
+ 334
A 11,330
B 11,328
C 11,200
D 9989
E None of these

4   844
+ 67
F 1011
G 911
H 912
J 801
K None of these

8   0.06 + 284.2 =
F 204.14
G 284.26
H 290.2
J 284.602
K None of these

GO

ANSWER ROWS **A** Ⓐ Ⓑ Ⓒ Ⓓ Ⓔ   **1** Ⓐ Ⓑ Ⓒ Ⓓ Ⓔ   **3** Ⓐ Ⓑ Ⓒ Ⓓ Ⓔ   **5** Ⓐ Ⓑ Ⓒ Ⓓ Ⓔ   **7** Ⓐ Ⓑ Ⓒ Ⓓ Ⓔ
B Ⓕ Ⓖ Ⓗ Ⓙ Ⓚ   **2** Ⓕ Ⓖ Ⓗ Ⓙ Ⓚ   **4** Ⓕ Ⓖ Ⓗ Ⓙ Ⓚ   **6** Ⓕ Ⓖ Ⓗ Ⓙ Ⓚ   **8** Ⓕ Ⓖ Ⓗ Ⓙ Ⓚ

9

$4\frac{1}{7} + 1\frac{3}{7} =$

A $2\frac{5}{7}$
B $4\frac{4}{7}$
C $5\frac{2}{7}$
D $5\frac{4}{7}$
E None of these

14

267.18
$+ \ 78.22$

F 345.16
G 345.36
H 344.5
J 345.44
K None of these

10

$^-8 + 9 =$

F $^-8$
G $^-9$
H 17
J 1
K None of these

15

$\frac{1}{5}$
$+ \ \frac{7}{10}$

A 1
B $1\frac{2}{5}$
C $1\frac{6}{7}$
D $\frac{9}{10}$
E None of these

11

$7\frac{3}{6} + 4\frac{4}{5} =$

A $3\frac{1}{6}$
B $11\frac{7}{11}$
C $11\frac{3}{10}$
D $12\frac{3}{10}$
E None of these

16

$2.3 + .6 + 1 =$

F 3.36
G 3.9
H 3.63
J 1.7
K None of these

12

$0.882 + 0.086 \ =$

F 0.8888
G 0.968
H 0.986
J 0.8906
K None of these

17

$\frac{2}{15} + \frac{1}{15} =$

A $\frac{7}{15}$
B $\frac{1}{3}$
C $\frac{2}{5}$
D $\frac{1}{5}$
E None of these

13

$8\frac{1}{4}$
$+ \ \frac{1}{8}$

A $8\frac{1}{8}$
B $9\frac{1}{8}$
C $8\frac{3}{8}$
D $9\frac{3}{8}$
E None of these

18

$.72$
$.38$
$+ \ .49$

F 1.59
G 1.6
H 1.49
J 1.5
K None of these

STOP

ANSWER ROWS   **9** Ⓐ Ⓑ Ⓒ Ⓓ Ⓔ   **11** Ⓐ Ⓑ Ⓒ Ⓓ Ⓔ   **13** Ⓐ Ⓑ Ⓒ Ⓓ Ⓔ   **15** Ⓐ Ⓑ Ⓒ Ⓓ Ⓔ   **17** Ⓐ Ⓑ Ⓒ Ⓓ Ⓔ
                10 Ⓕ Ⓖ Ⓗ Ⓙ Ⓚ   **12** Ⓕ Ⓖ Ⓗ Ⓙ Ⓚ   **14** Ⓕ Ⓖ Ⓗ Ⓙ Ⓚ   **16** Ⓕ Ⓖ Ⓗ Ⓙ Ⓚ   **18** Ⓕ Ⓖ Ⓗ Ⓙ Ⓚ

Example

Directions: Mark the space for the correct answer to each subtraction problem. Choose "NG" if the right answer is not given.

A		**A** 7.3
		B 5.3
6.2 − 1.1 =		**C** 4.9
		D 5.21
		E NG

B		**F** 36
		G 27
37		**H** 47
− 10		**J** 7
		K NG

If the right answer is not given, mark the space for "NG." This means "not given."

When you are not sure of an answer, check it by adding.

Practice

1

822
− 59

A 837
B 881
C 763
D 737
E NG

5

432.55 − 16.78 =

A 415.23
B 315.77
C 315.66
D 415.66
E NG

2

45,173
− 7,266

F 52,439
G 4212
H 37,903
J 37,907
K NG

6

67.29 − 8.726 =

F 57.56
G 57.566
H 58.566
J 58.564
K NG

3

19.02 − 0.26 =

A 18.76
B 19.76
C 19.28
D 18.226
E NG

7

3.772
− 2.006

A 5.778
B 1.766
C 32.778
D 1.774
E NG

4

7182
− 6793

F 489
G 389
H 1389
J 1611
K NG

8

27.08
− 0.08

F 27
G 27.16
H 26
J 26.88
K NG

GO

9

$$\frac{5}{8}$$
$$- \frac{1}{4}$$

A $\frac{1}{8}$

B $\frac{1}{4}$

C $\frac{3}{4}$

D $\frac{7}{8}$

E NG

14

$$\frac{8}{8}$$
$$- \frac{2}{8}$$

F $\frac{1}{16}$

G $\frac{3}{4}$

H $\frac{4}{3}$

J $\frac{1}{2}$

K NG

10

$$\frac{11}{12} - \frac{1}{2} =$$

F $\frac{1}{12}$

G $1\frac{5}{12}$

H $\frac{5}{12}$

J $\frac{1}{4}$

K NG

15

$$^{-}2 - 6 =$$

A $^{-}8$

B $^{-}4$

C 4

D 8

E NG

11

$$8\frac{7}{8} - \frac{3}{4} =$$

A $8\frac{1}{4}$

B $7\frac{1}{2}$

C $8\frac{1}{8}$

D 7

E NG

16

$$13\frac{4}{15} - 7\frac{1}{3} =$$

F 6

G $6\frac{14}{15}$

H $7\frac{1}{3}$

J $7\frac{1}{15}$

K NG

12

$$5$$
$$- 1\frac{4}{9}$$

F $3\frac{5}{9}$

G $4\frac{5}{9}$

H $3\frac{1}{3}$

J $4\frac{2}{3}$

K NG

17

$$\frac{7}{9} - \frac{1}{3} = \square$$

A $1\frac{1}{9}$

B $\frac{2}{3}$

C $\frac{5}{18}$

D $\frac{4}{9}$

E NG

18

$$0.024$$
$$- 0.015$$

F 0.009

G 0.019

H 0.039

J 0.1245

K NG

13

$$28.75$$
$$- 0.79$$

A 28.96

B 28.07

C 27.04

D 27.96

E NG

STOP

ANSWER ROWS   **9** Ⓐ Ⓑ Ⓒ Ⓓ Ⓔ   **12** Ⓕ Ⓖ Ⓗ Ⓙ Ⓚ   **15** Ⓐ Ⓑ Ⓒ Ⓓ Ⓔ   **17** Ⓐ Ⓑ Ⓒ Ⓓ Ⓔ
10 Ⓕ Ⓖ Ⓗ Ⓙ Ⓚ   **13** Ⓐ Ⓑ Ⓒ Ⓓ Ⓔ   **16** Ⓕ Ⓖ Ⓗ Ⓙ Ⓚ   **18** Ⓕ Ⓖ Ⓗ Ⓙ Ⓚ
11 Ⓐ Ⓑ Ⓒ Ⓓ Ⓔ   **14** Ⓕ Ⓖ Ⓗ Ⓙ Ⓚ

Example

Directions: Mark the space for the correct answer to each multiplication problem. Choose "NH" if the right answer is not given.

A			A 3.5

A

$\begin{array}{r} 1.3 \\ \times\ 2.2 \\ \hline \end{array}$

A 3.5
B 2.62
C 28.6
D 2.86
E NH

B

$4 \times \frac{1}{2} =$

F $\frac{1}{2}$
G 2
H $2\frac{1}{4}$
J 8
K NH

 **Tips**

If the right answer is not given, mark the space for "NH." This means "not here."

Remember to place the decimal point correctly.

Practice

1

$\begin{array}{r} 4.07 \\ \times\ 3.29 \\ \hline \end{array}$

A 13.3903
B 133.903
C 13.393
D 123.903
E NH

5

$400 \times 0.725 =$

A 400.725
B 280.75
C 29
D 290
E NH

2

$\frac{5}{6} \times 6 =$

F 30
G 36
H 4
J 6
K NH

6

$\begin{array}{r} 6.92 \\ \times\ 0.418 \\ \hline \end{array}$

F 2.89256
G 2.9
H 28.9256
J 7.338
K NH

3

$\begin{array}{r} 5.47 \\ \times\ 3.6 \\ \hline \end{array}$

A 196.92
B 19.692
C 19.697
D 9.07
E NH

7

$(8)\,(^-4)\,(1)$

A 35
B $^-1$
C $^-32$
D 0
E NH

4

$20\%\ \text{of}\ 50 =$

F 52
G 25
H 100
J 10
K NH

8

$\begin{array}{r} 480 \\ \times\ 325 \\ \hline \end{array}$

F 480,325
G 156,000
H 15,600
J 156,325
K NH

ANSWER ROWS **A** Ⓐ Ⓑ Ⓒ Ⓓ Ⓔ **1** Ⓐ Ⓑ Ⓒ Ⓓ Ⓔ **3** Ⓐ Ⓑ Ⓒ Ⓓ Ⓔ **5** Ⓐ Ⓑ Ⓒ Ⓓ Ⓔ **7** Ⓐ Ⓑ Ⓒ Ⓓ Ⓔ
  B Ⓕ Ⓖ Ⓗ Ⓙ Ⓚ **2** Ⓕ Ⓖ Ⓗ Ⓙ Ⓚ **4** Ⓕ Ⓖ Ⓗ Ⓙ Ⓚ **6** Ⓕ Ⓖ Ⓗ Ⓙ Ⓚ **8** Ⓕ Ⓖ Ⓗ Ⓙ Ⓚ

9

$\frac{4}{7} \times \frac{3}{8} =$

A $4\frac{1}{8}$
B 1
C $\frac{21}{32}$
D $\frac{3}{14}$
E NH

10

$(2 \times 5) + 9 =$

F 18
G 23
H 47
J 810
K NH

11

28
x 79

A 2217
B 2212
C 1212
D 1472
E NH

12

$2\frac{2}{3} \times 5 =$

F $13\frac{1}{3}$
G $12\frac{2}{5}$
H 43
J $10\frac{2}{3}$
K NH

13

$1\frac{1}{5} \times 3\frac{1}{2} =$

A $3\frac{4}{5}$
B $4\frac{1}{2}$
C $4\frac{1}{5}$
D $\frac{3}{10}$
E NH

14

28% of $45 =

F $13.40
G $73.00
H $28.45
J $12.60
K NH

15

$^-12 \times {}^-7 =$

A $^-$84
B 84
C $^-$72
D 72
E NH

16

$(2 + 4)\, 3^2 =$

F 38
G 36
H 18
J 45
K NH

17

30% of □ = 24

A 54
B 8
C 125
D 80
E NH

18

$(12 - 6)\,(2 + 9) =$

F 66
G 7
H 17
J 60
K NH

19   15 is what percent of 60?

A 45%
B 25%
C 2.5%
D 75%
E NH

STOP

ANSWER ROWS   **9** Ⓐ Ⓑ Ⓒ Ⓓ Ⓔ   **12** Ⓕ Ⓖ Ⓗ Ⓙ Ⓚ   **15** Ⓐ Ⓑ Ⓒ Ⓓ Ⓔ   **18** Ⓕ Ⓖ Ⓗ Ⓙ Ⓚ
10 Ⓕ Ⓖ Ⓗ Ⓙ Ⓚ   **13** Ⓐ Ⓑ Ⓒ Ⓓ Ⓔ   **16** Ⓕ Ⓖ Ⓗ Ⓙ Ⓚ   **19** Ⓐ Ⓑ Ⓒ Ⓓ Ⓔ
11 Ⓐ Ⓑ Ⓒ Ⓓ Ⓔ   **14** Ⓕ Ⓖ Ⓗ Ⓙ Ⓚ   **17** Ⓐ Ⓑ Ⓒ Ⓓ Ⓔ

Example

Directions: Mark the space for the correct answer to each division problem. Choose "N" if the right answer is not given.

A		
$0.2\overline{)12}$	**A** 10	
	B 24	
	C 6	
	D N	

B		
$\frac{1}{9} \div \frac{5}{9} =$	**F** $\frac{9}{5}$	
	G 9	
	H $\frac{1}{5}$	
	J N	

If the right answer is not given, mark the space for "N." This means the answer is not given.

Watch out! It's easy to make mistakes when dividing fractions and decimals, so be extra careful when you work with them.

Practice

1 $6.702 \div 10 =$

A 67.02
B 0.6702
C 10.6702
D N

5 $9\overline{)67}$

A 7 R4
B 7
C 6 R1
D N

2 $400\overline{)2800}$

F 8
G 70
H 7
J N

6 $^-480 \div 8 =$

F 60
G $^-60$
H $^-80$
J N

3 $16 \div \frac{4}{5} =$

A $12\frac{4}{5}$
B 64
C 45
D N

7 $4\overline{)0.076}$

A 19
B 0.29
C 0.0019
D N

4 $.18\overline{).54}$

F 3
G .3
H .03
J N

8 $1200 \div 9\frac{7}{8}$ is closest in value to

F 15
G 12
H 120
J N

ANSWER ROWS
A Ⓐ Ⓑ Ⓒ Ⓓ   1 Ⓐ Ⓑ Ⓒ Ⓓ   3 Ⓐ Ⓑ Ⓒ Ⓓ   5 Ⓐ Ⓑ Ⓒ Ⓓ   7 Ⓐ Ⓑ Ⓒ Ⓓ
B Ⓕ Ⓖ Ⓗ Ⓙ   2 Ⓕ Ⓖ Ⓗ Ⓙ   4 Ⓕ Ⓖ Ⓗ Ⓙ   6 Ⓕ Ⓖ Ⓗ Ⓙ   8 Ⓕ Ⓖ Ⓗ Ⓙ

9

$\frac{14}{-2} =$

A $^-7$
B 28
C 6
D N

10

$32\overline{)676}$

F $23\frac{2}{3}$
G 23
H $21\frac{1}{8}$
J N

11 $(20 + 34) \div 9 + (7 - 5) =$

A 11
B 8
C 4
D N

12

$\frac{5}{8} + \frac{1}{4} =$

F $\frac{5}{12}$
G $2\frac{1}{4}$
H 1
J N

13

$\frac{9}{10} \div 9 =$

A $\frac{1}{10}$
B $\frac{1}{9}$
C 10
D N

14

$^-60 \div 6 =$

F 6
G 10
H $^-10$
J N

15

$\frac{-32}{-8} =$

A 24
B 4
C $^-4$
D N

16 $[50 - (37 - 17)] \div 10 =$

F 10
G 30
H 3
J N

17

$17\overline{)250}$

A 12 R14
B 14 R8
C 16
D N

18

$67.23 \div 10 =$

F 6.723
G 670.23
H 672.3
J N

19

$50\overline{)7502}$

A 15 R2
B 150 R2
C 16
D N

20

$\frac{3}{14} \div \frac{2}{5} =$

F $6\frac{3}{14}$
G $1\frac{1}{70}$
H $\frac{3}{35}$
J N

STOP

ANSWER ROWS
9 Ⓐ Ⓑ Ⓒ Ⓓ   12 Ⓕ Ⓖ Ⓗ Ⓙ   15 Ⓐ Ⓑ Ⓒ Ⓓ   18 Ⓕ Ⓖ Ⓗ Ⓙ
10 Ⓕ Ⓖ Ⓗ Ⓙ   13 Ⓐ Ⓑ Ⓒ Ⓓ   16 Ⓕ Ⓖ Ⓗ Ⓙ   19 Ⓐ Ⓑ Ⓒ Ⓓ
11 Ⓐ Ⓑ Ⓒ Ⓓ   14 Ⓕ Ⓖ Ⓗ Ⓙ   17 Ⓐ Ⓑ Ⓒ Ⓓ   20 Ⓕ Ⓖ Ⓗ Ⓙ

Lesson 9   Test Yourself

Examples   **Directions:** Read and work each problem. Find the correct answer. Mark the space for your choice.

E1

$^-10 \div 2 =$

A $^-5$
B 12
C 5
D $^-6$
E None of these

E2

$(6 - 2) \times 3 =$

F 0
G 6
H 10
J 11
K None of these

1

$600 \times 12.3 =$

A 73.8
B 738
C 612.3
D 7380
E None of these

2

$7.392 - 1.64 =$

F 6.332
G 5.752
H 9.032
J 6.752
K None of these

3

$\begin{array}{r} 914.03 \\ + \quad 55.627 \\ \hline \end{array}$

A 969.657
B 1069.657
C 969.633
D 858.403
E None of these

4

$0.6\overline{)7.44}$

F 1.24
G 1.224
H 0.24
J 12.4
K None of these

5

25% of 48 =

A 12.25
B 14
C 12.5
D 13
E None of these

6

$\frac{1}{9} \times \frac{3}{4} =$

F $\frac{3}{37}$
G $\frac{1}{3}$
H $\frac{9}{4}$
J $\frac{1}{12}$
K None of these

7

$^-6 - 5 =$

A 1
B $^-11$
C $^-1$
D 30
E None of these

8

$10 + ^-12 =$

F $^-2$
G 22
H 2
J 10
K None of these

9   45 is 15% of what number?

A 30
B 150
C 300
D 350
E None of these

GO

ANSWER ROWS   **E1** Ⓐ Ⓑ Ⓒ Ⓓ Ⓔ   **2** Ⓕ Ⓖ Ⓗ Ⓙ Ⓚ   **5** Ⓐ Ⓑ Ⓒ Ⓓ Ⓔ   **8** Ⓕ Ⓖ Ⓗ Ⓙ Ⓚ

E2 Ⓕ Ⓖ Ⓗ Ⓙ Ⓚ   **3** Ⓐ Ⓑ Ⓒ Ⓓ Ⓔ   **6** Ⓕ Ⓖ Ⓗ Ⓙ Ⓚ   **9** Ⓐ Ⓑ Ⓒ Ⓓ Ⓔ

1 Ⓐ Ⓑ Ⓒ Ⓓ Ⓔ   **4** Ⓕ Ⓖ Ⓗ Ⓙ Ⓚ   **7** Ⓐ Ⓑ Ⓒ Ⓓ Ⓔ

10

$$10$$
$$- 5\frac{7}{8}$$

F $6\frac{1}{10}$

G $6\frac{4}{7}$

H $5\frac{4}{7}$

J $5\frac{1}{11}$

K None of these

11

$$\frac{3}{100} + \frac{3}{10} =$$

A 1.3

B 0.09

C 0.33

D 1.6

E None of these

12

$$7 \times {}^{-}2 \times 4 =$$

F 56

G 42

H $^{-}56$

J $^{-}36$

K None of these

13

$$8\overline{)3216}$$

A 402

B 42

C 337

D 307

E None of these

14

$$7 + .9 + 5.8 =$$

F 12.17

G 9.22

H 8.17

J 13.7

K None of these

15

$$\frac{5}{7} - \frac{3}{14} =$$

A $\frac{1}{2}$

B $\frac{5}{14}$

C $\frac{8}{21}$

D $\frac{3}{7}$

E None of these

16

$$388$$
$$614$$
$$+ \; 275$$

F 1176

G 1266

H 1167

J 1277

K None of these

17

$$38.2 - 19 =$$

A 57.2

B 20.2

C 19.8

D 19

E None of these

18 What is 60% of 55?

F 30

G 5

H 105

J 33

K None of these

19

$$\frac{3}{16} \div \frac{5}{8} = \square$$

A 1

B $\frac{3}{10}$

C 5

D $\frac{5}{8}$

E None of these

20

$$9\frac{5}{8}$$
$$+ \; 4\frac{3}{8}$$

F $13\frac{7}{8}$

G $5\frac{2}{8}$

H 14

J $15\frac{1}{8}$

K None of these

STOP

UNIT 3   Applications

Lesson 10   Geometry

Example   **Directions:** Find the correct answer to each geometry problem.
Mark the space for your choice.

A What shape will be formed if you fold the square on the right in half two times on the dashed lines?

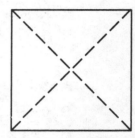

   A a triangle

   B a square

   C a trapezoid

   D a pentagon

 **You can solve many problems without computing. For these problems, it is especially important to look for key words, numbers, and figures to help you find the correct answer.**

Practice

1 Look at the two squares below. What is the area of the shaded portion of the larger square?

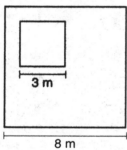

   A 64 m²

   B 9 m²

   C 55 m²

   D 25 m²

2 An angle of 110° is

   F obtuse

   G acute

   H right

   J similar

3 Which of these is a hexagon?

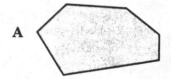

A

B

C

D

122

GO

ANSWER ROWS   **A** Ⓐ Ⓑ Ⓒ Ⓓ   **1** Ⓐ Ⓑ Ⓒ Ⓓ   **2** Ⓕ Ⓖ Ⓗ Ⓙ   **3** Ⓐ Ⓑ Ⓒ Ⓓ

4 Which of these angles is about 70°?

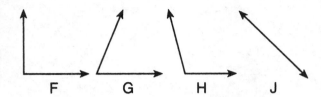

F   F
G   G
H   H
J   J

5 Which line below has a length that is greater than the radius of the circle but less than its diameter?

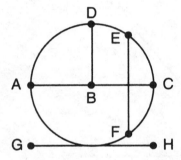

A $\overline{AC}$
B $\overline{BD}$
C $\overline{EF}$
D $\overline{GH}$

6

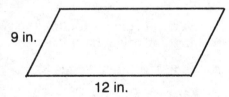

9 in.

12 in.

The perimeter of this parallelogram is —

F 108 in.
G 33 in.
H 21 in.
J 42 in.

7 A roof has an area of 660 square feet. Which of these shows the length and width of the roof?

A 60 ft by 60 ft
B 20 ft by 30 ft
C 66 ft by 100 ft
D 22 ft by 30 feet

8 What is the volume of this box?

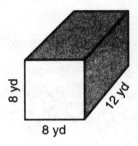

8 yd

12 yd

8 yd

F 156 cu. yd.
G 28 cu. yd.
H 640 cu. yd.
J 768 cu. yd.

9 The figure below is a cube. Which statement about the figure is true?

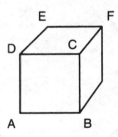

A Plane ABCD is perpendicular to plane CDEF.
B Plane ABCD is parallel to plane CDEF.
C The volume of the cube is equal to side AB times side AD.
D The volume of the cube is equal to plane ABCD times plane CDEF.

GO

10 Which of these statements would prove the triangle below is a right triangle?

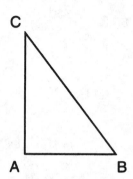

F ∠ CAB has a measure of 90°.

G $\overline{AB}$, $\overline{BC}$, and $\overline{CA}$ are equal in length.

H ∠ CAB has a measure greater than 90°.

J $\overline{BC}$ equals $\overline{AB}$ plus $\overline{AC}$.

11 The two figures below are similar. What is the length of side GH?

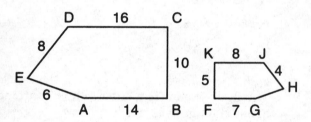

A 3 units

B 2 units

C 7 units

D 3.5 units

12 A carpenter has a piece of wood that is 24 inches long and 12 inches wide. She cut it in half exactly so she has two squares of wood. What is the perimeter of either of the squares of wood?

F 12 inches

G 144 inches

H 48 inches

J 60 inches

13 Which of these shows an angle?

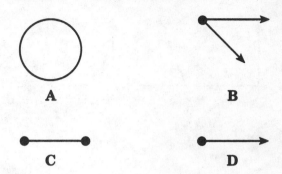

14 Which of these shows how to bisect a line segment?

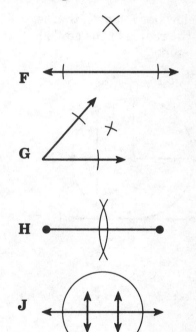

15 The general rule for finding the volume of a rectangular prism is —

A (Side 1 + Side 2 + Side 3)³

B Face 1 x Face 2 x Face 3

C Side 1 + Side 2 + Side 3

D Side 1 x Side 2 x Side 3

GO

16 Look at the rectangle below. Suppose you cut the shaded section out of the rectangle. What would the perimeter of the new shape be?

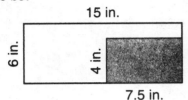

15 in.

6 in.

4 in.

7.5 in.

F 42 inches

G 31.5 inches

H 60 inches

J 32.5 inches

17 Which of these shapes are congruent?

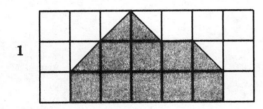

1

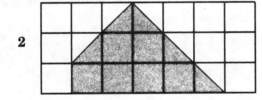

2

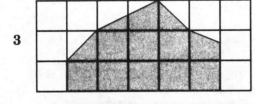

3

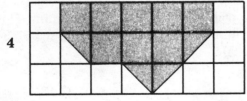

4

A 2 and 4

B 2 and 3

C 1 and 2

D 1 and 4

18 Which of these is an obtuse angle?

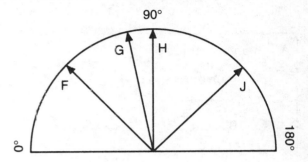

90°

G H

F J

0° 180°

F F

G G

H H

J J

19 Which solid figure has only 4 faces that are equal in size?

A a cube

B a pyramid

C a cone

D a rectangular prism

20 Which statement is true about this figure?

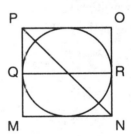

P   O

Q   R

M   N

F The length of a side of the square is the same as the diameter of the circle.

G The perimeter of the square and the circumference of the circle are the same.

H Diagonal PN is the same as the diameter of the circle.

J The length of a side of the square is the same as the radius of the circle.

STOP

Lesson 11   Measurement

Example   **Directions:** Find the correct answer to each measurement problem. Mark the space for your choice.

A In a yard, there are —

   A 40 inches

   B 3 meters

   C 100 centimeters

   D 3 feet

B Math class starts at 10:15 and ends 55 minutes later. What time does it end?

   F 11:10

   G 10:55

   H 11:05

   J 11:55

Sometimes a problem will have information you do not need to find the answer. You should ignore this information.

Before you mark your answer choice, ask yourself, "Does this answer make sense?"

Practice

1 The students in a class are making a scale drawing of their school. The scale they are using is 1 inch = 4 feet. When they drew the cafeteria, their drawing was 22 inches long and 18 inches wide. What were the real dimensions of the cafeteria?

   A 22 feet by 18 feet

   B 4 feet by 40 feet

   C 88 feet by 72 feet

   D 26 feet by 22 feet

2 A gardener bought a kilogram of fertilizer for house plants. He used $\frac{1}{2}$ of the fertilizer. How many grams of fertilizer did he have left?

   F 500 grams

   G 1000 grams

   H 0.5 grams

   J 50 grams

3 Antonio had 2 quarters, 2 dimes, and 4 nickels. He bought a hamburger for $.69, but didn't have enough to buy a double-burger, which was $1.19. How much change did Antonio receive?

   A $.39

   B $.29

   C $.50

   D $.21

4 During a winter day in Colorado, the temperature at 6:00 in the morning was ⁻12°. It reached 35° at 1:30, and then dropped to 21° at 7:00 in the evening. How far did the temperature drop from 1:30 to 7:00?

   F 33°

   G 14°

   H 47°

   J 21°

GO

5 Which of these statements is correct?

A A bed is about 10 feet long.

B A basketball rim is a little more than 3 yards high.

C A football field is about 1000 meters long.

D An adult is about 100 centimeters tall.

6 In planning a vacation trip, Cal and Doris saw that the map had a scale on which $\frac{1}{2}$ inch represented a mile. On the map, the distance from the freeway to the theme park was 5 inches. What is the actual distance from the highway to the park?

F 2.5 miles

G 7 miles

H 5 miles

J 10 miles

7 Which of these represents the greatest mass?

A 1.5 kilograms

B 150 grams

C 2000 milligrams

D 0.2 kilograms

8 Carla leaves her home at 7:30 and arrives at work about 8:15. She finishes work at 5:00, but it takes her 15 minutes longer to drive home than it does to drive to work. How much time does Carla spend commuting to and from work each day?

F 1 hour and 30 minutes

G 2 hours

H 1 hour and 45 minutes

J 2 hours and 30 minutes

9 Cassius works in a paint store. He is mixing a special blend for a customer that required 2 liters of basic white, 200 milliliters of blue tint, and 450 milliliters of yellow tint. How much paint did he mix all together? (1 liter = 1000 milliliters)

A 2650 milliliters

B 2650 liters

C 26,500 milliliters

D 0.0265 liters

10 What fraction of a gallon is 1 pint?

F $\frac{1}{4}$

G $\frac{1}{8}$

H $\frac{1}{2}$

J $\frac{3}{4}$

11 About how big is a paperback book?

A 6 inches by 10 inches

B 12 inches by 18 inches

C 2 inches by 4 inches

D 4 inches by 7 inches

12 Which of these temperatures is the warmest?

F ⁻27°

G ⁻72°

H 0°

J ⁻12°

13 Suppose you had 8 coins that totaled $.40. Which of these statements could be true?

A One of them could be a quarter.

B None of them could be pennies.

C None of them could be nickels.

D At least one must be a penny.

Example   **Directions:** Find the correct answer to each problem. Mark the space for your choice.

A There are 5 vowels in the English alphabet. What is the ratio of vowels to consonants?

   A $\frac{1}{26}$

   B $\frac{1}{5}$

   C $\frac{5}{21}$

   D $\frac{5}{26}$

B What is the total cost of a shirt if the price is $20.00 and the tax is 5%?

   F $21.00

   G $19.00

   H $15.00

   J $25.00

Read the question carefully. Sometimes it will be necessary to take several steps to find the right answer.

If you are sure you know which answer choice is correct, just fill in the space and move on to the next problem.

Practice

1 Suppose you know the price of a gallon of gasoline. What else must you know to find out how much it will cost to fill a car's gas tank?

   A The speed of the car

   B The distance the car will be driven

   C The distance the car has been driven

   D The number of gallons the tank will hold

2 This chart shows how much it costs to send packages of different weights. How much would it cost to send a package that weighed 8 pounds and 7 ounces?

First pound	$6.00
2 to 5 pounds	$9.00
Each additional pound	$2.00 per pound

   F $17.00

   G $2.00

   H $9.00

   J $13.00

3 Dave had 30 baseball trading cards. He traded $\frac{1}{2}$ of them for a new glove. He then traded $\frac{1}{5}$ of what he had left for an autographed baseball. How many cards did he trade for the baseball?

   A 6

   B 5

   C 3

   D 15

4 A cube has 6 sides. Half are red and half are blue. If you roll the cube, what are the odds that a red side will be facing up?

   F $\frac{1}{6}$

   G $\frac{1}{2}$

   H $\frac{2}{3}$

   J $\frac{2}{1}$

GO ⟩

This table shows the number of students in the seventh grade of a school who were born in each month. Use the table to answer questions 5 through 7.

Month of Birth	Number of Students
JAN	12
FEB	15
MAR	21
APR	19
MAY	20
JUN	17
JUL	16
AUG	18
SEP	14
OCT	10
NOV	7
DEC	4

5 In which three months were the most students born?

A January, February, and March

B May, June, and July

C March, April, and May

D October, November, and December

6 What is the average number of students born during August, September, and October?

F 14

G 12

H 42

J 11

7 How many more students were born in the month with the greatest number of births than in the month with the fewest births?

A 20

B 16

C 21

D 17

8 How much change would you get from a $20 bill if you bought a pair of running socks for $3.49 and shorts for $12.75?

F $16.51

G $3.76

H $7.25

J $10.74

This graph shows how a doctor spends her day. Use it to answer questions 9 – 11.

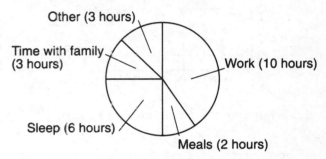

9 What fractional part of the day does the doctor spend at work?

A $\frac{1}{10}$

B $\frac{5}{12}$

C $\frac{1}{2}$

D $\frac{7}{12}$

10 What percentage of the day does the doctor spend with the family?

F 8.5%

G 30%

H 3%

J 12.5%

11 How much time does the doctor spend doing things other than working or sleeping?

A 10 hours

B 9 hours

C 8 hours

D 16 hours

GO

The graph below shows the number of people who attended a county fair in 1991 and 1992. Use the graph to answer questions 12 through 14.

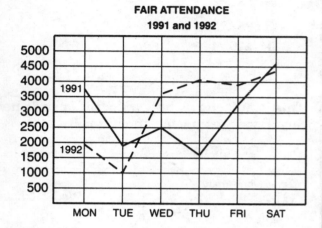

FAIR ATTENDANCE
1991 and 1992

12 What was the attendance at the fair on Wednesday in 1991?

F 3600
G 2500
H 2000
J 1400

13 About how many more people attended the fair on Thursday in 1992 than on the same day in 1991?

A 4000
B 1500
C 500
D 2500

14 The fair will earn a profit when attendance is more than 3000. What is the total number of days in both years in which the attendance was greater than 3000?

F 3
G 4
H 7
J 9

15 When Mr. Walker went shopping for a new computer, he found that the computer he wanted ranged in price from $1750 to $2000. He decided to buy a computer with a price in the middle of the range. How much does he expect to pay for the computer?

A $125
B $1975
C $1775
D $1825

16 Software for the computer includes an operating system ($59.00), a word processor ($129.00), and a graphics program ($159.00). What is the total cost of this software?

F $347
G $447
H $118
J $229

17 A printer for the computer costs $450.00. It will be on sale in a month for 20% less. How much will he save by waiting a month to buy the printer?

A $540
B $360
C $90
D $20

18 In order to run some programs, Mr. Walker will have to add memory to his computer. Memory chips, which contain 1 million bytes of memory, cost $43 each. The computer now has 2 million bytes of memory, but Mr. Walker needs 8 million. How much will it cost to add the memory chips he needs?

F $344
G $258
H $96
J $248

GO ▷

For numbers 19 through 22, choose the number sentence you would use to solve each problem.

19 Tina's best time for the marathon is 4 hours and 10 minutes. To qualify for the state championship, she must run the marathon in 3 hours and 50 minutes or better. How much must her time improve for her to qualify for the championship?

A $3 + 50 - \square = 4 + 10$

B $4 + 10 - \square = 3 + 50$

C $(4 \times 60) + 10 - \square = (3 \times 60) + 50$

D $(4 \times 60) - \square = (3 \times 60) + 50$

20 Suppose the sales tax in a state was 5%. How can you figure the total cost of a car if the price is $12,000 plus tax?

F $(.05 \times \$12,000) = \square$

G $\$12,000 - (.05 \times \$12,000) = \square$

H $\$12,000 + .05 = \square$

J $\$12,000 + (.05 \times \$12,000) = \square$

21 A highway crew can paint 6.5 miles of highway line in a day. How much line can they paint in 2.6 days?

A $6.5 \times 2.6 = \square$

B $6.5 \div 2.6 = \square$

C $6.5 - 2.6 = \square$

D $6.5 + 2.6 = \square$

22 A research laboratory has a supply of distilled water in 10-liter bottles. The total number of bottles in the laboratory is 2540. How much distilled water does the laboratory have in all?

F $10 \times \square = 2540$

G $2540 \times 10 = \square$

H $2540 \div 10 = \square$

J $2540 + 10 = \square$

23 How much will it cost to buy 15 cans of juice if the price is 4 cans for $1.60?

A $60.00

B $6.00

C $6.40

D $19.00

Use this graph to do questions 24 and 25.

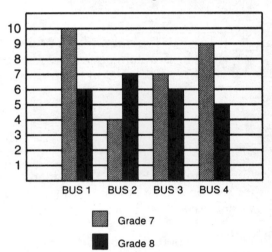

Students Riding a School Bus

24 What is the total number of seventh graders who ride the buses?

F 30

G 24

H 20

J 31

25 A family moved into the school district with a pair of twins in eighth grade and one child in seventh grade. The new students will ride bus 2. How many seventh and eight graders will now ride bus 2?

A 9 seventh graders and 5 eighth graders

B 8 seventh graders and 9 eighth graders

C 8 seventh graders and 10 eighth graders

D 5 seventh graders and 9 eighth graders

STOP

ANSWER ROWS   19 Ⓐ Ⓑ Ⓒ Ⓓ   21 Ⓐ Ⓑ Ⓒ Ⓓ   23 Ⓐ Ⓑ Ⓒ Ⓓ   25 Ⓐ Ⓑ Ⓒ Ⓓ

20 Ⓕ Ⓖ Ⓗ Ⓙ   22 Ⓕ Ⓖ Ⓗ Ⓙ   24 Ⓕ Ⓖ Ⓗ Ⓙ

Example   **Directions:** Find the correct answer to each algebra problem. Mark the space for your choice.

A What rule is used to change the "Input" numbers in this table to "Output" numbers?

  A add $^-6$

  B add $^+6$

  C multiply by $^-2$

  D multiply by $^+7$

Input	Output
$^-3$	$^+3$
$^-2$	$^+4$
$^-1$	$^+5$
$^-0$	$^+6$
1	$^+7$

 **If the answer you find is not one of the answer choices, read the problem again and rework it. If you still can't find the correct answer, skip the problem and come back to it later.**

Practice

1 Which statement is true about the number that goes in the box to make the number sentence true?

$$500 \times \square = 5215$$

  A The number is between 9 and 10.

  B The number is exactly 10.

  C The number is less than 9.

  D The number is greater than 10.

2 A package of cat food weighs 5 pounds. Jackie feeds her cat 4 ounces of food a day. To see how long a bag of food will last, Jackie uses the equation below:

$$(5 \times 16) \div 4 = n$$

What does the n represent?

  F the number of ounces in 5 pounds

  G the number of days the food will last

  H the amount of food the cat eats each day

  J the weight of a bag of food

3 If $x - 100 = 50$, then $x =$

  A 150

  B 50

  C 5000

  D 500

4 Which equation means, "2 times a number is less than 3 times the same number"?

  F $(2 \times 3) < n$

  G $2 + n < 3 + n$

  H $2n < 3n$

  J $2n > 3n$

5 Which of these shows how to find the value of n for the equation $n \times 3 = 48$?

  A 3×48

  B $48 \div 3$

  C $3 + 48$

  D $48 - 3$

GO

---

6 What is the greatest whole number that makes this number sentence true?

$$16 + \square < 30$$

F 11

G 45

H 14

J 13

7 If n is a whole number, which of these statements is true?

A If $n - 4 = 7$, then $9 \div n = 3$.

B If $n + 4 = 7$, then $3 \div n = 3$.

C If $n + 4 = 7$, then $9 \div n = 3$.

D If $n + 7 = 4$, then $9 \div 3 = n$.

8 If $5 > a$ and $a > b$, what should replace the circle in the expression $5 \bigcirc b$?

F $<$

G $>$

H $=$

J $-$

9 $7x - 8 = 20$

$$x =$$

A 4

B 12

C 1

D $^-1$

10 Which of these shows how to find the number of hours (h) in 5 days?

F $24 \times 5 = h$

G $24 + 5 = h$

H $24 - 5 = h$

J $24 \div 5 = h$

Use this graph to answer question 11.

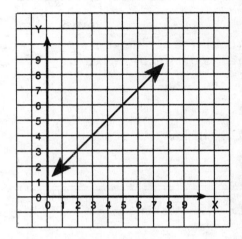

11 The line is the graph for —

A $y = x + 7$

B $y = 3x$

C $y = x$

D $y = x + 1$

12 If $\frac{3}{8} = \frac{x}{32}$, then $x =$

F 4

G 12

H 24

J 96

13 If x is a positive whole number, and $\frac{x}{20} = \frac{5}{x}$, then $x =$

A 30

B 4

C 10

D 5

STOP

ANSWER ROWS   **6** Ⓕ Ⓖ Ⓗ Ⓙ   **8** Ⓕ Ⓖ Ⓗ Ⓙ   **10** Ⓕ Ⓖ Ⓗ Ⓙ   **12** Ⓕ Ⓖ Ⓗ Ⓙ
              7 Ⓐ Ⓑ Ⓒ Ⓓ   **9** Ⓐ Ⓑ Ⓒ Ⓓ   **11** Ⓐ Ⓑ Ⓒ Ⓓ   **13** Ⓐ Ⓑ Ⓒ Ⓓ

Examples   **Directions:** Read and work each problem. Find the correct answer. Mark the space for your choice.

E1

What is the perimeter of a square with an area of 100 square inches?

A 100 inches

B 40 inches

C 10 inches

D 25 inches

E2

How much change would you get from a $5.00 bill if you bought items for $2.95?

F $3.95

G $7.95

H $3.05

J $2.05

---

1   If $x \div 12 = 4$, then $x =$

A   3

B   16

C   48

D   412

2   Jason is helping his parents paint his room. He began with 1 gallon of paint and used 3 pints. How many pints did he have left?

F   5 pints

G   4 pints

H   7 pints

J   11 pints

3   What is the volume of the rectangular prism shown below?

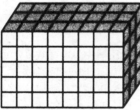

= 1 cubic unit

A   40 cubic units

B   120 cubic units

C   16 cubic units

D   130 cubic units

4   What is the radius of a circle if the diameter is equal to 20?

F   40

G   20 x 20 x π

H   20π

J   10

5   Look at the game board below. Suppose you closed your eyes and dropped a coin on the board. What are the chances the coin would land on a black square?

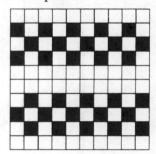

A $\frac{1}{5}$

B $\frac{3}{1}$

C $\frac{3}{10}$

D $\frac{1}{4}$

6   Which of these is the greatest volume?

F   1500 milligrams

G   15 kilograms

H   1500 grams

J   15 centigrams

GO

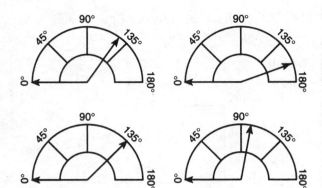

7   Which statement is true about the angles shown above?

   A   Only one angle is a right angle.

   B   Two of the angles are obtuse.

   C   All the angles are acute.

   D   All the angles are obtuse.

8   A number N is half of 120. Which equation shows this problem?

   F $2 \times N = 120$

   G $\frac{1}{2} \times N = 120$

   H $N \times 120 = \square$

   J $\frac{1}{2} + N = 120$

9   The figure below shows an isosceles triangle inscribed within a circle. Line CE is vertical to line AB. Which angle has the same measure as angle *BAC*?

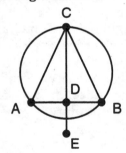

   A   angle *BCA*

   B   angle *ABC*

   C   angle *ADE*

   D   angle *BCE*

10   Which unit would you probably use to measure the distance from one city to another?

   F   kilometers

   G   meters

   H   centimeters

   J   millimeters

11   A moving company charges $2.00 for each 100 pounds of weight to be moved. Which number sentence shows how to find the cost of moving 5000 pounds of furniture?

   A $(5000 \times 100) \div \$2.00 = \square$

   B $(5000 - 100) \times \$2.00 = \square$

   C $(5000 \div 100) \times \$2.00 = \square$

   D $5000 \times 100 \times \$2.00 = \square$

12   Carly's family has a wood burning stove. They began the winter with 1 cord of wood. After 5 weeks, they had $\frac{3}{8}$ of a cord left. Which number sentence shows how much wood they burned?

   F $1 + \square = \frac{3}{8}$

   G $1 - \square = \frac{3}{8}$

   H $\frac{3}{8} - \square = 1$

   J $1 \div 5 = \square$

13   A mountain bike normally sells for $400. This week it is on sale for 20% less. What is the total cost of the bike if sales tax is 5%?

   A $420

   B $399

   C $320

   D $336

GO

Use the graph below to do numbers 14 and 15.

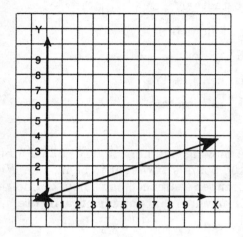

14 Which equation does the line represent?

F $y = x \div 3$

G $y = x + 3$

H $y = 3 - x$

J $y = x - 6$

15 If x were equal to 12, what would y be?

A 6

B 36

C 9

D 4

16 Jamie's test scores are shown in the box below. What is Jamie's average score?

$$94, 89, 87, 82, 91, 88$$

F 87.1

G 91.125

H 88

J 88.5

17 All of the angles in the figure below are 90°. What is the area of the figure?

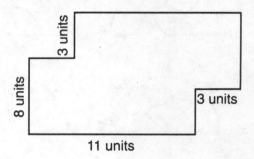

A 154 units ^{2}

B 148 units ^{2}

C 50 units ^{2}

D 136 units ^{2}

18 Which of these statements about the value of a group of coins is correct?

F A group of 3 coins could equal 10¢

G A group of 6 coins could equal $2

H A group of 6 coins could equal $1

J A group of 6 coins could equal 10¢

19 The schedule below shows a family's plan to visit a museum. Based on the schedule, how long do they plan to spend in the Native American Exhibit?

8:00   Leave home
8:50   Arrive at museum. Begin in the African Tribal Art wing.
10:15   Religious Art of the Far East
11:00   19th Century American Illustrations
12:00   Lunch
12:45   Native American Exhibit
1:50   Leave museum. Spend 45 minutes in outdoor sculpture garden.

A 70 minutes

B 55 minutes

C 1 hour and 5 minutes

D 45 minutes

GO

20 Suppose you cut the shape below along the dotted lines. What shapes will you get?

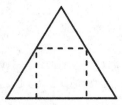

F Three triangles and a hexagon

G Six triangles

H Four triangles

J A square and three triangles

21 About how much does a baseball bat weigh?

A 1 ton

B 1 ounce

C 1 gram

D 1 kilogram

22 The workers in a company can assemble about 25 motors in an 8-hour shift. They normally work 40 hours in a week. The foreman uses the formula

$$(40 \div 8) \times 25 = n$$

What does n mean in the equation?

F The number of workers needed to assemble 25 motors

G The average time it takes to assemble a motor

H The number of motors the workers can assemble in a week

J The number of motors the workers can assemble in a day

The graph below shows how two different materials expand when they are heated. Use the graph to do numbers 23 through 25.

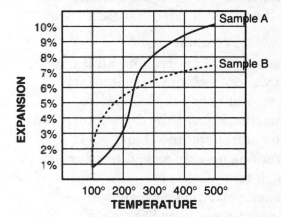

23 At 400°, how much has Sample A expanded?

A 8.5%

B 9.5%

C 9%

D 10%

24 At about what temperature have Sample A and Sample B expanded the same percentage?

F less than 200°

G exactly 200°

H between 200° and 250°

J between 250° and 300°

25 Based on the results shown on the graph, which of these statements is true?

A Sample B expands more rapidly than Sample A at low temperatures.

B Sample B expands more rapidly than Sample A at high temperatures.

C Sample A always expands faster than Sample B.

D Sample B always expands faster than Sample A.

STOP

To the Student:

These tests will give you a chance to put the tips you have learned to work.

A few last reminders…

- **Be sure you understand all the directions before you begin each test. You may ask the teacher questions about the directions if you do not understand them.**
- **Work as quickly as you can during each test.**
- **When you change an answer, be sure to erase your first mark completely.**

- You can guess at an answer or skip difficult items and go back to them later.
- Use the tips you have learned whenever you can.
- It is OK to be a little nervous. You may even do better.

Now that you have completed the lessons in this unit, you are on your way to scoring high!

STUDENT'S NAME			SCHOOL
LAST	FIRST	MI	TEACHER
			FEMALE ○ MALE ○

BIRTHDATE

MONTH	DAY	YEAR

GRADE

⑤   ⑥   ⑦   ⑧   ⑨   ⑩

PART 1   CONCEPTS

E1 Ⓐ Ⓑ Ⓒ Ⓓ	4 Ⓕ Ⓖ Ⓗ Ⓙ	9 Ⓐ Ⓑ Ⓒ Ⓓ	14 Ⓕ Ⓖ Ⓗ Ⓙ	18 Ⓕ Ⓖ Ⓗ Ⓙ	22 Ⓕ Ⓖ Ⓗ Ⓙ
E2 Ⓕ Ⓖ Ⓗ Ⓙ	5 Ⓐ Ⓑ Ⓒ Ⓓ	10 Ⓕ Ⓖ Ⓗ Ⓙ	15 Ⓐ Ⓑ Ⓒ Ⓓ	19 Ⓐ Ⓑ Ⓒ Ⓓ	23 Ⓐ Ⓑ Ⓒ Ⓓ
1 Ⓐ Ⓑ Ⓒ Ⓓ	6 Ⓕ Ⓖ Ⓗ Ⓙ	11 Ⓐ Ⓑ Ⓒ Ⓓ	16 Ⓕ Ⓖ Ⓗ Ⓙ	20 Ⓕ Ⓖ Ⓗ Ⓙ	24 Ⓕ Ⓖ Ⓗ Ⓙ
2 Ⓕ Ⓖ Ⓗ Ⓙ	7 Ⓐ Ⓑ Ⓒ Ⓓ	12 Ⓕ Ⓖ Ⓗ Ⓙ	17 Ⓐ Ⓑ Ⓒ Ⓓ	21 Ⓐ Ⓑ Ⓒ Ⓓ	25 Ⓐ Ⓑ Ⓒ Ⓓ
3 Ⓐ Ⓑ Ⓒ Ⓓ	8 Ⓕ Ⓖ Ⓗ Ⓙ	13 Ⓐ Ⓑ Ⓒ Ⓓ			

PART 2   COMPUTATION

E1 Ⓐ Ⓑ Ⓒ Ⓓ Ⓔ	3 Ⓐ Ⓑ Ⓒ Ⓓ Ⓔ	7 Ⓐ Ⓑ Ⓒ Ⓓ Ⓔ	11 Ⓐ Ⓑ Ⓒ Ⓓ Ⓔ	15 Ⓐ Ⓑ Ⓒ Ⓓ Ⓔ	19 Ⓐ Ⓑ Ⓒ Ⓓ Ⓔ
E2 Ⓕ Ⓖ Ⓗ Ⓙ Ⓚ	4 Ⓕ Ⓖ Ⓗ Ⓙ Ⓚ	8 Ⓕ Ⓖ Ⓗ Ⓙ Ⓚ	12 Ⓕ Ⓖ Ⓗ Ⓙ Ⓚ	16 Ⓕ Ⓖ Ⓗ Ⓙ Ⓚ	20 Ⓕ Ⓖ Ⓗ Ⓙ Ⓚ
1 Ⓐ Ⓑ Ⓒ Ⓓ Ⓔ	5 Ⓐ Ⓑ Ⓒ Ⓓ Ⓔ	9 Ⓐ Ⓑ Ⓒ Ⓓ Ⓔ	13 Ⓐ Ⓑ Ⓒ Ⓓ Ⓔ	17 Ⓐ Ⓑ Ⓒ Ⓓ Ⓔ	21 Ⓐ Ⓑ Ⓒ Ⓓ Ⓔ
2 Ⓕ Ⓖ Ⓗ Ⓙ Ⓚ	6 Ⓕ Ⓖ Ⓗ Ⓙ Ⓚ	10 Ⓕ Ⓖ Ⓗ Ⓙ Ⓚ	14 Ⓕ Ⓖ Ⓗ Ⓙ Ⓚ	18 Ⓕ Ⓖ Ⓗ Ⓙ Ⓚ	22 Ⓕ Ⓖ Ⓗ Ⓙ Ⓚ

PART 3   APPLICATIONS

E1 Ⓐ Ⓑ Ⓒ Ⓓ	4 Ⓕ Ⓖ Ⓗ Ⓙ	9 Ⓐ Ⓑ Ⓒ Ⓓ	14 Ⓕ Ⓖ Ⓗ Ⓙ	19 Ⓐ Ⓑ Ⓒ Ⓓ	24 Ⓕ Ⓖ Ⓗ Ⓙ
E2 Ⓕ Ⓖ Ⓗ Ⓙ	5 Ⓐ Ⓑ Ⓒ Ⓓ	10 Ⓕ Ⓖ Ⓗ Ⓙ	15 Ⓐ Ⓑ Ⓒ Ⓓ	20 Ⓕ Ⓖ Ⓗ Ⓙ	25 Ⓐ Ⓑ Ⓒ Ⓓ
1 Ⓐ Ⓑ Ⓒ Ⓓ	6 Ⓕ Ⓖ Ⓗ Ⓙ	11 Ⓐ Ⓑ Ⓒ Ⓓ	16 Ⓕ Ⓖ Ⓗ Ⓙ	21 Ⓐ Ⓑ Ⓒ Ⓓ	26 Ⓕ Ⓖ Ⓗ Ⓙ
2 Ⓕ Ⓖ Ⓗ Ⓙ	7 Ⓐ Ⓑ Ⓒ Ⓓ	12 Ⓕ Ⓖ Ⓗ Ⓙ	17 Ⓐ Ⓑ Ⓒ Ⓓ	22 Ⓕ Ⓖ Ⓗ Ⓙ	27 Ⓐ Ⓑ Ⓒ Ⓓ
3 Ⓐ Ⓑ Ⓒ Ⓓ	8 Ⓕ Ⓖ Ⓗ Ⓙ	13 Ⓐ Ⓑ Ⓒ Ⓓ	18 Ⓕ Ⓖ Ⓗ Ⓙ	23 Ⓐ Ⓑ Ⓒ Ⓓ	

Part 1   Concepts

Examples   **Directions:** Read and work each problem. Find the correct answer. Mark the space for your choice.

E1

Which of these decimals is less than 1.833 and greater than 0.974?

A 0.896

B 1.194

C 1.841

D 0.093

E2

What is another way to write 20,000,000 + 1,000,000 + 10,000, + 800 + 4?

F   218,004

G 211,100,804

H 21,010,804

J 20,110,804

---

1 A fisherman was measuring the depth of a stream with a stick. In May it was $\frac{3}{5}$ of the way up the stick, in June it was $\frac{2}{3}$, in July it was $\frac{1}{2}$, and in August it was $\frac{7}{9}$. In which month was the water the deepest?

A May

B June

C July

D August

2 Which of these number sentences could be used to find the missing number in the pattern below?

1, 2, 3, 5, 8, 13, 21, 34, ___ , 89

F 34 + 13 = 47

G 34 − 13 = 21

H 21 + 34 = 55

J 89 − 21 = 68

3 Which of the following is another name for $\frac{8}{5}$?

A $1\frac{3}{5}$

B $\frac{16}{12}$

C $3\frac{1}{5}$

D $\frac{5+3}{8}$

4 Which of these is a factor of 18, 45, and 72?

F 8

G 9

H 5

J 6

5 Which point on this number line is $\frac{2}{5}$?

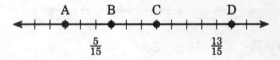

A A

B B

C C

D D

6 Which of these is the best estimate of the percentage of the circle that is shaded?

F 85%

G 50%

H 25%

J 10%

GO

7 What should replace the box in the equation

$$58,291 = 50,000 + \square + 200 + 90 + 1$$

A   8

B   80

C   800

D   8000

8 Which of these is the best estimate of

$$19.87 \times 4\frac{11}{12}$$

F   20 x 4

G   19 x 4

H   20 x 5

J   19 x 5

9 $7^2 - 12 =$

A   37

B   5

C   0

D   61

10 Look at the figure below. What fraction of the box is shaded?

F $\frac{7}{16}$

G $\frac{3}{8}$

H $\frac{1}{2}$

J $\frac{2}{3}$

11 Which of these is another way to write 0.92?

A   9.2%

B   .092%

C   920%

D   92%

12 How many of the numbers in the box below will be 100,000 when rounded to the nearest ten-thousand?

| 108,639 | 86,174 | 96,310 | 112,581 |

F   1

G   2

H   3

J   4

13 Which of these is not another way to write $\frac{7}{28}$?

A $\frac{14}{56}$

B   25%

C $\frac{1}{25}$

D   0.25

14 $3.7 \times 10^3 =$

F   370

G   3700

H   37,000

J   37

15 Which of these is 7 tenths more than 23.72?

A   27.72

B   23.727

C   24.42

D   23.42

141

GO

16 The 8 in 7.2084 means —

F $\frac{8}{100}$

G $\frac{8}{10,000}$

H $\frac{8}{10}$

J $\frac{8}{1000}$

17 8103.57 ÷ 52.0189 is between—

A 5 and 80

B 10 and 100

C 100 and 1000

D 1000 and 10,000

18 $\sqrt{144}$

F 8

G 10

H 14

J 12

19 What does the *n* in the equation below stand for?

$$(n + 3) \times 10 = (10 \times 4) + (10 \times 3)$$

A 4

B 3

C 7

D 70

20 What number should appear in the last circle if the pattern below is continued?

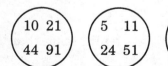

F 26

G 75

H 72

J 98

21 Which group below contains both a prime number and a composite number?

A 28 and 57

B 13 and 47

C 39 and 67

D 105 and 121

22 A store sold $44,832.89 worth of goods on Saturday. The manager told the owner they did about $45,000 worth of business. To what place value did the manager round the total sales?

F tens

G thousands

H ones

J hundreds

23 What are the largest and the smallest 5-digit numbers you can make with the digits 2, 9, 0, 5, and 7?

A 20,579 and 97,520

B 20,579 and 97,502

C 25,079 and 97,502

D 29,570 and 97,250

24 Which of these is six ten-thousandths?

F 0.0060

G 0.0600

H 0.6000

J 0.0006

25 If $x > 500$ and $x < 520$, which of the following is a possible value of x?

A 529

B 494

C 502

D 607

STOP

Examples   **Directions:** Find the correct answer to each problem. Choose "None of these" if the correct answer is not given.

E1

$^-1 + 7 =$

A   0
B   6
C $^-8$
D   17
E   None of these

E2

$\frac{1}{3} \times 36 =$

F   6
G   8
H   14
J   13
K   None of these

1

$260\overline{)208}$

A   .06
B   6
C   8
D   .8
E   None of these

6

$8 \times 5 + 3 =$

F   120
G   853
H   34
J   64
K   None of these

2

$\begin{array}{r} 7.226 \\ + \ .899 \\ \hline \end{array}$

F   8.125
G   7.673
H   7.125
J   6.327
K   None of these

7

$\begin{array}{r} 5602 \\ - \ 629 \\ \hline \end{array}$

A   527
B   6231
C   5027
D   4973
E   None of these

3

$\begin{array}{r} 19040 \\ - \ 7391 \\ \hline \end{array}$

A   12649
B   2351
C   11649
D   26431
E   None of these

8

$\begin{array}{r} 1.58 \\ \times \ 1.07 \\ \hline \end{array}$

F   2.406
G   11.587
H   1.6906
J   1.5856
K   None of these

4

$^-70 \times 2 =$

F   702
G $^-140$
H   68
J   140
K   None of these

9

$16\overline{)732}$

A   42
B $52\frac{5}{8}$
C $45\frac{3}{4}$
D   46
E   None of these

5

$5\frac{3}{5} \div 7 =$

A $\frac{3}{5}$
B   4
C $1\frac{1}{3}$
D $\frac{4}{5}$
E   None of these

10

$70\% \text{ of } 45 =$

F   31.5
G   30.5
H   70.45
J   3.15
K   None of these

GO

11

$2\frac{4}{9} + 2\frac{4}{9} =$

A $4\frac{9}{4}$
B $4\frac{8}{18}$
C $5\frac{1}{9}$
D $4\frac{4}{9}$
E   None of these

12

$3 \times 12 + 9 =$

F   45
G   61
H   38
J   144
K   None of these

13

$100.02 - 0.08 =$

A   100.04
B   100.06
C   92.2
D   99.94
E   None of these

14

$\frac{-70}{-35} =$

F $^-2$
G   2
H   4
J $^-35$
K   None of these

15

$\frac{21}{30} + \frac{24}{30} =$

A $\frac{1}{10}$
B $\frac{3}{4}$
C $1\frac{1}{2}$
D $15\frac{1}{30}$
E   None of these

16

$7\frac{4}{5} - 5\frac{1}{2} =$

F $13\frac{1}{10}$
G $2\frac{3}{7}$
H $1\frac{3}{5}$
J $2\frac{3}{10}$
K   None of these

17

$\begin{array}{r} 3002 \\ + 215 \\ \hline \end{array}$

A   3213
B   32,125
C   32,152
D   3217
E   None of these

18

$59.174 - .482 =$

F   58.312
G   59.312
H   59.692
J   58.629
K   None of these

19

$620 \times .001 =$

A   .62
B   62
C   6.2
D   62.1
E   None of these

20

$\frac{7}{8} = \frac{\square}{40}$

F   5
G   8
H   35
J   28
K   None of these

21 $3 \times (15 \div 5 + 4) - 8 =$

A   12
B $^-3$
C   5
D   13
E   None of these

22   4 is what percent of 16?

F   4%
G   25%
H   64%
J   50%
K   None of these

144

STOP

Examples   **Directions:** Read and work each problem. Find the correct answer. Mark the space for your choice.

E1

What is the average weight of three people who weigh 152, 160, and 147 pounds?

A 156

B 149.5 pounds

C 152.67 pounds

D 153 pounds

E2

What is the surface area of a cube if an edge is 5 centimeters long?

F 600 cm²

G 120 cm²

H 150 cm²

J 200 cm²

---

1 What will be the coordinates of point B if you move triangle ABC 4 units to the right?

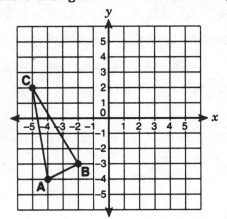

A $(1, ^-3)$

B $(2, ^-3)$

C $(^-6, ^-6)$

D $(2, 2)$

2 If $19y = 76$, then $y =$

F 57

G 4

H 95

J 3

3 An angle of 76° is —

A symmetric

B right

C obtuse

D acute

4 The distance around a city park is 1200 yards. Which of these could be the length and width of the park?

F 400 yards and 200 yards

G 120 yards and 100 yards

H 600 yards and 200 yards

J 400 yards and 600 yards

5 In which of these situations would you need an exact number?

A Finding the number of students in a school

B Taking a census of the people in the U.S.

C Learning how tall a mountain is

D Determining how much corn was harvested from a field

6 What is the perimeter of the shaded figure shown below?

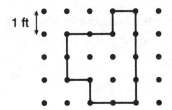

1 ft

F 6 ft

G 13 ft

H 14 ft

J 8 ft

GO

The chart below shows the number of cars that were parked on different streets at three times during the day. Use this chart to do numbers 7 through 9.

Parking Pattern			
Street	9 - 10	12 - 1	4 - 5
Maple	15	9	6
Central	12	14	17
Main	18	20	22
West	6	4	5
East	4	3	6
Court	9	8	10
Broad	11	14	12
Total	75	72	78

7   The greatest number of cars were parked on —

A Main from 4 - 5

B Main from 12 - 1

C Central from 4 - 5

D Maple from 9 - 10

8   The total number of cars parked on Broad Street during the three periods was —

F 25

G 37

H 26

J 36

9   The average number of cars parked on the streets during the three time periods was —

A 78

B 76

C 75

D 74.6

10   Which of these is the coldest temperature?

F 0°

G 32°

H −7°

J −2°

11   The Outdoor Adventure Club is planning a bike trip. Their goal is to ride an average of 50 miles a day during an 8 hour period. The trip will take 5 days and will cost an average of $22 per person per day. Using this information, which of these questions could you not answer?

A The total cost of the trip per day

B The total distance they will travel

C The average distance traveled in an hour

D The maximum speed per day

12   What is the area of square ABCD if the radius of the circle is 5 cm?

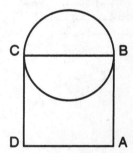

F 25 cm²

G 100 cm²

H 40 cm²

J 20 cm²

13   If x is a positive whole number, and $\frac{5}{x} = \frac{x}{80}$, then $x =$

A 20

B 50

C 160

D 25

GO

14 A construction crew is building a deck that is 20 feet by 40 feet. They have finished 200 square feet of the deck. What percentage of the deck is unfinished?

F 25%

G 20%

H 200%

J 75%

15 Which equation means, "A number multiplied by itself is 81"?

A $y^2 = 81$

B $y + y = 81$

C $y \times 81 = y$

D $y \times 0 = 81$

16 Pens from Store A are 6 for $8.40. The same pens from Store B are 8 for $9.60. How much would you save if you bought 12 pens from the store with the lower price?

F $14.40

G $16.80

H $2.40

J $1.20

17 What rule is used to change the "Input" numbers in this table to "Output" numbers?

Input	Output
+2	−4
+6	−12
−5	+10
−4	+8
+8	−16

A add −6

B add +8

C multiply by −2

D multiply by +2

18 Which angle is an obtuse angle?

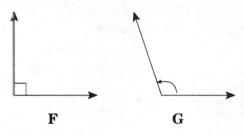

F   G

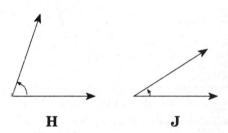

H   J

Use this coordinate graph to answer questions 19 and 20.

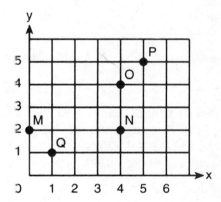

19 What point is at (4, 2)?

A Q

B M

C O

D N

20 What are the coordinates of point P?

F (4, 4)

G (5, 4)

H (5, 5)

J (4, 2)

The graph below shows the percentage of customers who prefer different flavors of ice cream. Use this graph to answer questions 21 through 23.

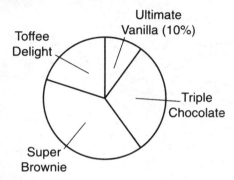

21 The percentage of customers who prefer Toffee Delight is twice that for Ultimate Vanilla. The percentage for Triple Chocolate is 1.5 times greater than Toffee Delight. What percentage of customers prefer Triple Chocolate?

A   15%

B   40%

C   30%

D   25%

22 To gather the information shown on the graph, the management of the ice cream store interviewed 500 customers. How many of them preferred Super Brownie?

F   200

G   400

H   350

J   300

23 Half of the customers who preferred Ultimate Vanilla made Triple Chocolate their second choice. If these customers had made Triple Chocolate their first choice, what would the new percentage be for Triple Chocolate?

A   45%

B   5%

C   15%

D   35%

24 What is the perimeter of this parallelogram?

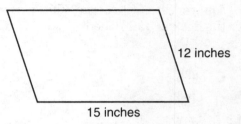

F   180 inches

G   42 inches

H   27 inches

J   54 inches

25 2500 grams =

A   0.25 kilograms

B   2.05 kilograms

C   2.5 kilograms

D   25 kilograms

26 If $x = 20$, then $3 + 4x =$

F   23

G   83

H   27

J   140

27 If you spin the spinner below 50 times, how many times will the arrow land on 1?

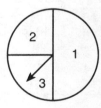

A   25

B   4

C   16

D   10

STOP

Answer Keys

Reading
Unit 1,
Vocabulary
Lesson 1-pg. 12

A	B
B	J
1	B
2	H
3	D
4	F
5	D
6	G
7	A
8	G

Lesson 2-pg. 13

A	A
B	H
1	C
2	G
3	A
4	J
5	C
6	F
7	B

Lesson 3-pg. 14

A	D
B	G
1	D
2	G
3	A
4	H
5	D
6	F
7	C
8	H

Lesson 4-pg. 15

A	C
B	F
1	A
2	H
3	D
4	J
5	C

Lesson 5-pg. 16

A	C
B	F
1	D
2	F
3	B
4	H
5	A
6	J

Lesson 6-pg. 17

A	B
B	J
1	A
2	H
3	D
4	G
5	B

Lesson 7-pgs. 18-21

E1	A
E2	H
1	C
2	J
3	B
4	G
5	D
6	H
7	B
8	F
9	A
10	J
11	B
12	J
13	C
14	F
15	C
16	J
17	A
18	J
19	B
20	J
21	B
22	H
23	C
24	J
25	A
26	J
27	D
28	H
29	D
30	G
31	A
32	J
33	B
34	H

Unit 2,
Comprehension
Lesson 8-pg. 22

A	A
1	D
2	H
3	B
4	F

Lesson 9-pgs. 23-26

A	B
1	D
2	F
3	C
4	G
5	B
6	F
7	C
8	H
9	A
10	H
11	D
12	G
13	D
14	F

Lesson 10-pgs. 27-32

A	C
1	D
2	G
3	D
4	G
5	D
6	F
7	A
8	H
9	D
10	J
11	B
12	G
13	B
14	G
15	D
16	G
17	D
18	F
19	C

Lesson 11-pgs. 33-41

E1	B
1	B
2	J
3	A
4	H
5	C
6	J
7	A
8	J
9	B
10	F
11	D
12	H
13	A
14	G
15	A
16	J
17	D
18	F
19	B
20	H
21	A
22	G
23	C
24	F
25	D
26	G
27	C
28	F
29	C
30	H
31	B

Test Practice
Part 1-pgs. 44-47

E1	A
E2	H
1	D
2	G

3 C
4 G
5 D
6 H
7 A
8 G
9 B
10 J
11 C
12 G
13 D
14 H
15 A
16 H
17 A
18 G
19 A
20 G
21 B
22 F
23 C
24 J
25 C
26 H
27 D
28 H
29 A
30 H
31 B
32 F
33 D
34 H

Test Practice
Part 2-pgs. 48-56
E1 A
1 C
2 F
3 B
4 J
5 B
6 H
7 A
8 G
9 D
10 F
11 C
12 J
13 B
14 G
15 C
16 F
17 D
18 H

19 C
20 G
21 C
22 J
23 B
24 G
25 A
26 H
27 D
28 F
29 A
30 J
31 A
32 G
33 D
34 J

Language
Unit 1, Language
Mechanics
Lesson 1-pgs. 58-59
A C
B J
1 C
2 F
3 B
4 G
5 D
6 F
7 C
8 F
9 D
10 F
11 C
12 J
13 B
14 H
15 D
16 F
17 B

Lesson 2-pgs. 60-62
A C
B J
1 B
2 F
3 C
4 F
5 D
6 H
7 D

8 F
9 C
10 G
11 C
12 G
13 B
14 F
15 A
16 H
17 B
18 F
19 C
20 J

Lesson 3-pgs. 63-66
E1 A
1 C
2 F
3 D
4 G
5 C
6 G
7 A
8 J
9 C
10 G
11 D
12 H
13 A
14 F
15 B
16 G
17 D
18 H
19 B
20 J
21 A
22 F
23 C
24 J
25 B
26 G
27 A
28 J
29 C

Unit 2
Lesson 4-pgs. 67-69
A C
B F
1 B
2 F
3 D
4 H

5 D
6 G
7 B
8 F
9 B
10 J
11 C
12 F
13 C
14 J
15 A
16 J
17 A
18 J
19 B
20 H

Lesson 5-pgs. 70-72
A B
B H
C C
1 A
2 H
3 C
4 G
5 C
6 H
7 A
8 J
9 B
10 H
11 B
12 H
13 A
14 J
15 A

Lesson 6-pgs. 73-76
A D
1 B
2 J
3 D
4 G
5 D
6 F
7 B
8 J
9 C
10 F
11 C
12 G
13 A
14 J

Lesson 7-pgs. 77-80

E1	B
1	D
2	H
3	A
4	G
5	D
6	H
7	B
8	J
9	B
10	F
11	B
12	G
13	C
14	F
15	C
16	J
17	D
18	F
19	D
20	G

Unit 3
Lesson 8-pgs. 81-82

A	B
B	H
1	D
2	F
3	A
4	H
5	B
6	G
7	D
8	F
9	E
10	G
11	D
12	F
13	C
14	G
15	A
16	G
17	B
18	J

Lesson 9-pgs.83-84

E1	D
E2	F
1	B
2	H
3	D
4	H

5	A
6	J
7	B
8	H
9	A
10	H
11	C
12	K
13	C
14	F
15	D
16	G
17	C
18	H
19	A
20	J

Unit 4
Lesson 10-pgs. 85-86

A	B
1	D
2	G
3	D
4	G
5	C
6	F
7	C
8	F
9	D

Lesson 11-pgs. 87-89

E1	D
E2	G
1	D
2	G
3	A
4	H
5	D
6	J
7	C
8	G
9	B
10	J
11	B
12	H
13	B
14	F
15	C
16	J
17	A

Test Practice,
Part 1-pgs. 92-94

E1	D

1	B
2	F
3	B
4	J
5	C
6	J
7	A
8	J
9	B
10	G
11	A
12	J
13	D
14	F
15	D
16	F
17	C
18	G
19	A
20	J
21	C

Test Practice,
Part 2-pgs. 95-98

E1	C
1	C
2	G
3	D
4	F
5	C
6	H
7	C
8	J
9	C
10	F
11	B
12	J
13	B
14	F
15	C
16	J
17	B
18	H
19	A
20	J

Test Practice,
Part 3-pgs. 99-100

E1	C
E2	H
1	C
2	J
3	A
4	J

5	C
6	H
7	B
8	F
9	C
10	J
11	D
12	K
13	C
14	H
15	B
16	F
17	D
18	G
19	B
20	F

Test Practice,
Part 4-pgs. 101-102

E1	B
1	D
2	F
3	D
4	G
5	A
6	H
7	B
8	F
9	C
10	H
11	B

Math
Unit 1, Concepts
Lesson 1-pgs. 104-105

A	D
B	H
1	C
2	G
3	A
4	J
5	B
6	J
7	C
8	F
9	B
10	H
11	C
12	G
13	A
14	H
15	D

Lesson 2-pgs. 106-107

A	A
B	J
1	B
2	J
3	A
4	G
5	C
6	J
7	B
8	H
9	A
10	H
11	C
12	F
13	D

Lesson 3-pgs. 108-109

A	A
B	H
1	D
2	H
3	B
4	F
5	A
6	H
7	D
8	G
9	B
10	H
11	C
12	H

Lesson 4-pgs. 110-111

E1	C
E2	J
1	D
2	J
3	A
4	G
5	A
6	H
7	D
8	J
9	A
10	F
11	C
12	G
13	C
14	G
15	A

Unit 2, Computation
Lesson 5-pgs. 112-113

A	B
B	K
1	E
2	J
3	A
4	G
5	D
6	H
7	A
8	G
9	D
10	J
11	D
12	G
13	C
14	K
15	D
16	G
17	C
18	F

Lesson 6-pgs. 114-115

A	E
B	G
1	C
2	J
3	A
4	G
5	E
6	J
7	B
8	F
9	E
10	H
11	C
12	F
13	D
14	G
15	A
16	K
17	D
18	F

Lesson 7-pgs. 116-117

A	D
B	G
1	A
2	K
3	B
4	J
5	D
6	F
7	C
8	G
9	D
10	K
11	B
12	F
13	C
14	J
15	B
16	K
17	D
18	F
19	B

Lesson 8-pgs. 118-119

A	D
B	H
1	B
2	H
3	D
4	F
5	A
6	G
7	D
8	H
9	A
10	H
11	B
12	J
13	A
14	H
15	B
16	H
17	D
18	F
19	B
20	J

Lesson 9-pgs. 120-121

A	A
B	K
1	D
2	G
3	A
4	J
5	E
6	J
7	B
8	F
9	C
10	K
11	C
12	H
13	A
14	J
15	A
16	J
17	E
18	J
19	B
20	H

Unit 3, Applications
Lesson 10-pgs. 122-125

A	A
1	C
2	F
3	A
4	G
5	C
6	J
7	D
8	J
9	A
10	F
11	A
12	H
13	B
14	H
15	D
16	F
17	D
18	J
19	B
20	F

Lesson 11-pgs. 126-127

A	D
B	F
1	C
2	F
3	D
4	G
5	B
6	J
7	A
8	H
9	A
10	G
11	D
12	H
13	A

Lesson 12-pgs. 128-131		Lesson 14-pgs. 134-137				Part 3-pgs. 145-148	
A	C	E1	B	13	C	E1	D
B	F	E2	J	14	G	E2	H
1	D	1	C	15	C	1	B
2	F	2	F	16	J	2	G
3	C	3	B	17	C	3	D
4	G	4	J	18	J	4	F
5	C	5	C	19	A	5	A
6	F	6	G	20	G	6	H
7	D	7	D	21	C	7	A
8	G	8	F	22	G	8	G
9	B	9	B	23	A	9	C
10	J	10	F	24	J	10	H
11	C	11	C	25	C	11	D
12	G	12	G			12	G
13	D	13	D	Part 2-pgs. 143-144		13	A
14	H	14	F	E1	B	14	J
15	D	15	D	E2	K	15	A
16	F	16	J	1	D	16	H
17	C	17	D	2	F	17	C
18	G	18	H	3	C	18	G
19	C	19	C	4	G	19	D
20	J	20	J	5	D	20	H
21	A	21	D	6	K	21	C
22	G	22	H	7	D	22	F
23	B	23	B	8	H	23	D
24	F	24	H	9	C	24	J
25	D	25	A	10	F	25	C
				11	E	26	G
				12	F	27	A
Lesson 13-pgs. 132-133				13	D		
A	B	Test Practice		14	G		
1	D	Part 1-pgs. 140-142		15	C		
2	G	E1	B	16	J		
3	A	E2	H	17	D		
4	H	1	D	18	K		
5	B	2	H	19	A		
6	J	3	A	20	H		
7	C	4	G	21	D		
8	G	5	B	22	G		
9	A	6	H				
10	F	7	D				
11	D	8	H				
12	G	9	A				
13	C	10	G				
		11	D				
		12	F				

Reading Progress Chart

Circle your score for each lesson. Connect your scores to see how well you are doing.

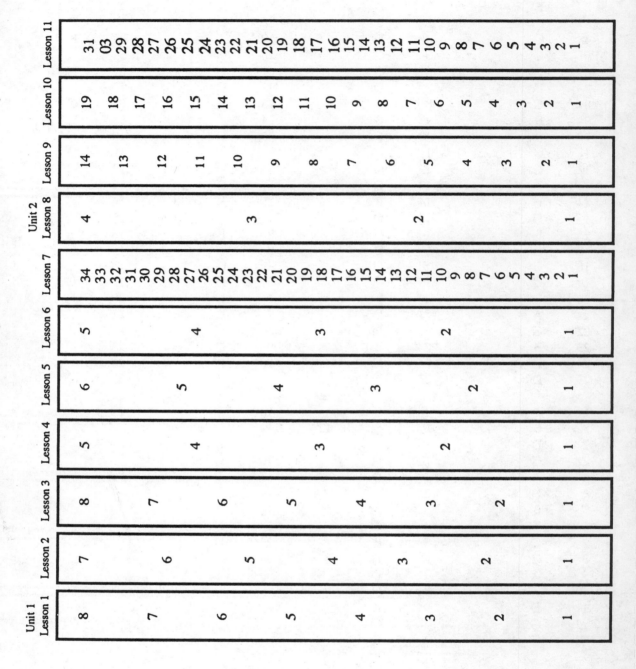

Unit 1 Lesson 1	Lesson 2	Lesson 3	Lesson 4	Lesson 5	Lesson 6	Lesson 7	Unit 2 Lesson 8	Lesson 9	Lesson 10	Lesson 11
8	7	8	5	6	5	34	4	14	19	31
						33			18	03
7	6	7	4	5	4	32		13	17	29
						31			16	28
						30			15	27
6	5	6		4	3	29	3	12	14	26
						28			13	25
5	4	5	3			27		11	12	24
						26			11	23
				3	2	25		10	10	22
						24				21
4	3	4	2			23	2	9	9	20
						22				19
				2		21		8	8	18
						20				17
						19			7	16
3	2	3				18		7		15
						17				14
						16		6	6	13
						15				12
						14			5	11
						13		5		10
						12				9
2		2				11			4	8
						10		4		7
						9				6
						8			3	5
						7		3		4
						6				3
1	1	1	1	1	1	5	1	2	2	2
						4				
						3				
						2		1	1	1
						1				

Language Progress Chart

Circle your score for each lesson. Connect your scores to see how well you are doing.

Unit 1 Lesson 1	Lesson 2	Lesson 3	Lesson 4	Lesson 5	Lesson 6	Lesson 7	Unit 2 Lesson 8	Lesson 9	Unit 3 Lesson 10	Lesson 11
17	20	29	20	15	14	20	18	20	9	17
16	19	27	19	14	13	19	17	19		16
15	18	26	18	13	12	18	16	18	8	15
14	17	25	17	12	11	17	15	17		14
13	16	24	16	11	10	16	14	16	7	13
12	15	23	15	10	9	15	13	15		12
11	14	22	14	9	8	14	12	14	6	11
10	13	21	13	8	7	13	11	13		10
9	12	20	12	7	6	12	10	12	5	9
8	11	19	11	6	5	11	9	11		8
7	10	18	10	5	4	10	8	10	4	7
6	9	17	9	4	3	9	7	9		6
5	8	16	8	3	2	8	6	8	3	5
4	7	15	7	2	1	7	5	7		4
3	6	14	6	1		6	4	6	2	3
2	5	13	5			5	3	5		2
1	4	12	4			4	2	4	1	1
	3	11	3			3	1	3		
	2	10	2			2		2		
	1	9	1			1		1		
		8								
		7								
		6								
		5								
		4								
		3								
		2								
		1								

Math Progress Chart

Circle your score for each lesson. Connect your scores to see how well you are doing.

Unit 1

Lesson 1	Lesson 2	Lesson 3	Lesson 4
15	13	12	15
14	12	11	14
13	11	10	13
12	10	9	12
11	9	8	11
10	8	7	10
9	7	6	9
8	6	5	8
7	5	4	7
6	4	3	6
5	3	2	5
4	2	1	4
3	1		3
2			2
1			1

Unit 2

Lesson 5	Lesson 6	Lesson 7	Lesson 8	Lesson 9	Lesson 10
18	18	19	20	20	20
17	17	18	19	19	19
16	16	17	18	18	18
15	15	16	17	17	17
14	14	15	16	16	16
13	13	14	15	15	15
12	12	13	14	14	14
11	11	12	13	13	13
10	10	11	12	12	12
9	9	10	11	11	11
8	8	9	10	10	10
7	7	8	9	9	9
6	6	7	8	8	8
5	5	6	7	7	7
4	4	5	6	6	6
3	3	4	5	5	5
2	2	3	4	4	4
1	1	2	3	3	3
		1	2	2	2
			1	1	1

Unit 3

Lesson 11	Lesson 12	Lesson 13	Lesson 14
13	25	13	25
12	24	12	24
11	23	11	23
10	22	10	22
9	21	9	21
8	20 19	8	20 19
7	18	7	18
6	17	6	17
5	16	5	16
4	15	4	15
3	14	3	14
2	13 12	2	13 12
1	11	1	11
	10		10
	9 8		9 8
	7		7
	6		6
	5 4		5 4
	3 2		3 2
	1		1